PATHWAYS TO THE SUPREME

PATHWAYS TO
THE SUPREME

Bede Griffiths

Edited by
Roland R. Ropers

HarperCollins*Publishers*

HarperCollins*Publishers*
77–85 Fulham Palace Road, London W6 8JB

First published in Great Britain
in 1995 by HarperCollins*Publishers*

1 3 5 7 9 10 8 6 4 2

Copyright © 1995 by Bede Griffiths

A catalogue record for this book is
available from the British Library

ISBN 000 627955 4

Printed and bound in Great Britain by
HarperCollinsManufacturing Glasgow

CONTENTS

INTRODUCTION

For many years it was my custom to copy out in a notebook passages which interested me in my reading in religion and philosophy. Over the years these passages came to fill two notebooks, and in looking them over I began to perceive a certain order, not only in my own personal experience but also in the growth of humanity. My interest focused for a long time on primitive religion, especially as described by Mircea Eliade in his *Patterns in Comparative Religion*. I began to see how all religion had grown from a perception of an all-pervading spirit which was held to be present in all phenomena – the earth, the sky, the water, the fire, the sun, the moon and the stars, in plants and trees and animals and in all human beings, but especially in any outstanding person or event, a king or a prophet or a seer, a storm or a volcano, in thunder and lightning, in mountains and hills, in great trees like cedars and in majestic animals like the lion or the elephant. This power was known by different names like *Mana* among the Melanesian islanders or *Wakan* among the American Indians, but often it came to be known simply as the *Great Spirit*. Above all, all these phenomena were seen as symbols of an invisible Spirit and the whole world was perceived as *sacred*, that is, the abode of invisible powers. St Paul was to speak of the Knowledge of God being seen in all creatures as his 'invisible power and divinity'. It was this sense of a power in nature which was felt to be above the world and to transcend humanity which gave rise to the idea of God.

But this power, though often conceived as one, was held to manifest itself in all these different forms, and these manifestations of the divine were conceived as gods and goddesses, angels and spirits, fairies and elves. The whole creation was full of these unseen presences, and this understanding was expressed in the form of myths and legends, stories of creation and destruction, of life and death, and especially of the ancestors and heroes of ancient times. It was from these myths, symbolic figures rising in the depths of the heart, which Jung called archetypes of the unconscious, that the religion of people of old was formed, creating a whole world which mirrored the human mind. But this sense of symbolism, of people and events symbolizing another world than that of the senses, is the source of all poetry. It was thus as Giambattista Vico (1668–1744), the Italian philosopher, observed that poetry always preceded prose, that people began to sing before they learned to calculate and record events. Poetry is essentially the capacity to symbolize reality, to see the world in terms of signs which make reality present. The rational mind abstracts ideas from concrete experience and forms systems of logical thought. The poetic mind mirrors reality itself in its concrete embodiment and expresses it in rhythmical form and concrete images.

My interest in my youth had always centred on poetry, especially the English romantic poets, Wordsworth, Shelley and Keats. It was they who taught me to look beyond the world of senses to the world beyond senses, the infinite and the eternal. Poets use language of symbolism which always points beyond the finite, temporal world to the infinite and eternal. It was Jacques Maritain and his wife Raissa, who taught me to see the link between poetry and mysticism. Maritain (1882–1973), Roman Catholic philosopher, was respected both for his interpretation of the thought of St Thomas Aquinas and for his own Thomist philosophy. Reared a Protestant, Maritain attended the Sorbonne in Paris where he was attracted by teachers who claimed that natural sciences alone could resolve human questions about life and death. There, however, he also met Raissa Oumansoff, a Russian-Jewish student, who began to share his quest for truth. Both became disillusioned with the Sorbonne's scientism and began to attend lectures by the intuitionist philosopher Henri Bergson. From him, they came to realize their need for 'the Absolute', and in 1906, two years after their marriage, they converted to Catholicism.

Both poetry and mysticism spring from the depths of the soul beyond the senses, but whereas the poet seeks to embody his experience of this inner mystery in words and images, the mystic seeks to go beyond word and thought to experience the hidden mystery from which all words and thoughts are derived. So from my study of primitive religion with its rich mythology, and poetry with its imaging the mystery which lies behind the outer world, I was led to philosophy, especially the philosophy of Plato. Plato saw beyond the world of senses to what he called 'the world of ideas'. For him the world which we perceive through our senses is an image, a reflection of a world which is invisible, infinite and eternal. In Plotinus, the neo-Platonist, the philosophy was developed to its supreme achievement in the concept of the *nous*, the mind in which all phenomena are reflected and which itself depends on an inner source, a transcendent mystery which can only be known in ecstasy, when the mind goes beyond all images and concepts, and experiences the one Reality from which the whole creation comes.

Plotinus was to have a profound influence on Christianity through St Augustine and the Greek Fathers, who were all Platonists, as well as on the Sufi mystics of Islam. But Platonism itself is only a reflection in the West of the long tradition of mystical philosophy in the East. Starting from the Vedas with their profound sense of a cosmic order – *rita* – underlying the universe, Indian philosophers were led to see in *Brahman*, the ground of all existence and in the *Atman*, the inner self, the ground of all consciousness and so to rise to the understanding of *Sat-Chit-Ananda*, being (*sat*) known in pure consciousness (*chit*) leading to absolute bliss (*ananda*). This is perhaps, the most profound conception of God, or of absolute Reality, which had ever been expressed.

At the same time Gautama Siddhartha, the Buddha, piercing through the outer world of the senses, which is always subject to change and decay, was able to experience the transcendent mystery of *nirvana*, which he expressed in negative terms, as the 'blowing out', the passing away of all phenomena and the awareness of the *void* (*sunyata*), that which remains when all images and concepts have been surpassed and the mind dwells in the silent depths of its original being. But Buddha's teaching was never merely speculative. He taught a method – the eightfold noble path – by which the human mind could pass beyond its limitations in the world of sense experience and natural desire to the experience of the absolute reality, which has no name or form. it is to this transcendence of sense experience, of images and concept, that all philosophy must lead us, until we enter into the depths of the Divine Mystery and know beyond all knowing.

It was this Divine Mystery, known by primitive people from the beginning and expressed in myth and poetry, and then developed in philosophical reflection, which came to be revealed in the Bible. The God of Israel was at first a tribal god who led his people to victory in battle and overcame all their enemies. Later he was conceived as a thunder-god, dwelling in the darkness of the clouds above Mount Sinai. But in the course of time the Hebrew prophets were able to rise above the concepts of a primitive tribal god to conceive a creator-god, who made heaven and earth and created all things by the power of his Word and his Spirit. Yet this creator-god always remained separate from his creation. His essential attribute was 'holiness', which meant literally separation. He was separate from the earth and the heavens and from all mankind whom he ruled by his power and his wisdom. But this God was also a God of justice and mercy, who demanded justice on the part of his people, the code of justice being contained in the Ten Commandments and in the Book of the Law. This conception of a moral order, not only a cosmic order as in the Vedas, or an impersonal moral order as in the Buddhist Dharma, but of an absolute, transcendent order of justice and truth, which was personal in character, was the distinctive revelation made to Israel. The God of Israel was a person in the sense of an infinite, eternal being, who conceived the world in his wisdom and brought it forth by the power of the will, which was a will of absolute Justice but also of Mercy and Love. This was the most exalted conception of a supreme God which was ever conceived.

But there remained a problem with the God of Israel. He was infinitely just and holy, the creator of all, but he was 'separate' from his creation. This led to a sense of human sin, of separateness from God, and later under Persian influence, to the concept of Satan, an evil spirit opposed to God. There was therefore a profound dualism in the religion of Israel. God was separate from humanity, and humanity from God, the world was divided between the good and the evil, the holy people of God and the world of the nations who were separated from God. The dualism also extended to the separation of the male from the female, and the rejection of all feminine forms of God found among the surrounding nations. The God of Israel was a patriarchal God opposed to all the forms of the Mother Goddess in matriarchal religion. Finally according to the religion of Israel the 'righteous' were to be separated from the 'wicked' and eternal punishment awaited the wicked, while the just were to enjoy eternal bliss.

This was the religion from which Christianity emerged. Jesus was proclaimed as the Messiah, the anointed king of Israel, who was to redeem his people from their sins and to establish his kingdom over the whole world. He was called Son of Man like the son of man in the apocalypse of Daniel who was to receive a kingdom and power over all peoples. He was also seen as the Son of God, of whom it was said in the psalm, 'Thou art my son, this day have I begotten thee'. He came to be regarded as the son of David, the child born of a virgin who had been prophesied by Isaiah. But he was also seen as the 'suffering servant' of Isaiah, who was to offer his life in sacrifice to redeem his people. Of what Jesus himself said we know nothing, as he preached in Aramaic in the synagogues and among the people in Galilee and no record of this has survived. His story and teaching were handed down in the Christian communities of people who had come to believe in him, above all the stories of the resurrection, in which Jesus had appeared after his death to eleven disciples. These stories were recorded first of all by St Paul within twenty years after the event, and in more detail by the evangelists, who collected the stories and teaching of Jesus which had come down through the churches and interpreted them in the light of their own experience. What we have in the four gospels therefore is the story of Jesus and his teaching translated into Greek from the Aramaic and interpreted by the evangelists in the light of their own experience at the end of the first century.

This must naturally make us cautious as to how we interpret the gospels today. We can see that the story of Jesus has undergone continuous reinterpretation. Each evangelist has his own point of view, derived normally from the community in which he was living, which had received the story from the apostles and the early teachers in the Church. We can see, moreover, a continual growth in the understanding of the Gospel. Matthew wrote from a Jewish perspective, seeing Jesus as the fulfillment of the prophecies of the Old Testament. Mark, writing probably from Rome, the centre of the Greco-Roman world, writes from a more ecumenical perspective, seeing Jesus as a 'divine man', performing miracles of healing and setting people free from subservience to the law. Luke writes as a Hellenist, a Greek-speaking convert, familiar with the traditions and customs of the Roman Empire, and completing the story of Jesus with the Acts of the Apostles, showing how the message of the Gospel was carried from Jerusalem to Rome.

But it is in the fourth gospel, attributed to the apostle John, that the full development of the Gospel study is found. Scholars generally agree that it was not written by John, the son of Zebedee, but another disciple, who calls himself the 'beloved disciple'. Whoever he was, he showed an insight into the mystical dimension of the life and teaching of Jesus which is not to be found in the earlier gospels. Written at the end of the first century it shows how reflection on the life and teaching of Jesus had led to a deeper understanding of the hidden mystery of Jesus. John sees Jesus as manifesting the Word of God, the Divine Wisdom, which had been with God from the beginning. This word is the source of life and the light which enlightens everyone who comes into the world. The Gospel is thus taken out of its limited Jewish setting and given a universal meaning. The life of Jesus is also seen in symbolic terms. It thus joins the ancient tradition of symbolic wisdom in which all the events of space and time are seen as reflections of a transcendent mystery which is beyond human understanding. The heart of John's gospel is the assertion that this Divine Mystery, this eternal Word has 'become flesh' as the person of Jesus of Nazareth. For John, Jesus of Nazareth is a human being, of whom he reveals facts which are not known to the other evangelists, but at the same time the Divine Mystery itself, the Word and Wisdom of God, revealed in the whole creation is present in Jesus in such a way that he can speak of himself as '*son of the Father*', that is, as reflecting in himself the divine light and communicating the divine spirit.

Thus the Divine Mystery, which had been known to humanity from the beginning as the Great Spirit pervading the universe, and had been conceived in India as the *Brahman*, the universal ground of being and as *Atman*, the universal ground of consciousness and in Buddhism as *Nirvana* and *sunyata*, the void, the abyss beyond all being, was revealed in Jesus as a human being, who revealed not only the Wisdom of God, known in the intimacy of his being as the Father, the source of all being but also as the Love of God, revealed in the sacrifice of his life on the cross, of which the climax was the resurrection. In the resurrection Jesus passed beyond all forms and appearances in space and time. The appearances to the disciples in the resurrection were only appearances to confirm the faith in the reality of his transcending space and time and entering into the eternal reality of the divine being. As Jesus was to say to the apostle Thomas: 'Blessed are those who have not seen and have believed.'

This is the 'mystery' of Christ revealed in St John's gospel and later elaborated by St Paul, which has been the basis of Christian theology and mysticism. The Greek Fathers found in the concept of the logos a link with the logos or reason of the universe known to Heraclitus and the Stoics; and then in the philosophy of Plato were to find a means to interpret the whole gospel in the light of Plato's understanding of the present world as a 'copy' or 'shadow' of the eternal world beyond space and time revealed in the resurrection. Thus the gospel message has undergone a continual process of reinterpretation, first with the evangelists themselves and St Paul, then with the Greek and Latin fathers and the medieval scholastics. Now today we are able to interpret it in the light of Vedanta and Mahayana doctrine and also of the teaching of the Muslim Sufis. Thus from primitive religion through poetry, philosophy and theology we are able to come to mystical understanding, the wisdom which transcends word and thought and yet can be shown to have a basis in both poetry and philosophy. As an example of Christian mysticism I have taken Ruysbroeck, the Flemish mystic, a disciple of Meister Eckhart, who shows the deepest insight of all Christian mystics. This is the only occasion when I have departed from my notebooks, as I had originally given passages from Julian of Norwich, but beautiful as they are, I feel that Ruysbroeck is more fundamental.

Bede Griffiths
Shantigiri (Mount of Peace)
Kreuth, Tegernsee
Germany   April 1992

I

THE WAY OF THE
COSMIC REVELATION

From the very dawn of primitive culture men have attempted in however crude and symbolic a form to understand the laws of life and to adapt their social activity to their workings. But primitive man does not look upon the external world in the modern way as a passive or mechanistic system, a background for human energies, mere matter for the human mind to mould. He sees it as a living world of mysterious forces greater than his own, in the placation and service of which his life consists.

He is surrounded by mysterious powers which manifest themselves both in external nature and in his inner consciousness, in earth and sky, in beasts and plants, no less than in dreams and visions and in the spirits of the dead. Hence primitive religion is characterized by its universality and vagueness, and it is impossible to isolate a single definite type of religious belief as the source and starting point of the whole development.

The *Tinglit* (Indians) do not divide the universe

1

arbitrarily into so many quarters ruled by so many supernatural beings. On the contrary supernatural power impresses them as a vast immensity, one in kind and impersonal, inscrutable as to its nature, but whenever manifesting itself to men taking a personal and it might be said, a human personal form in whatever aspect it displays itself. Thus the sky spirit is the ocean of supernatural energy as it manifests itself in the sky, the bear spirit as it manifests itself in the bear, the rock spirit as it manifests itself in the rock . . . For this reason there is but one name for this spiritual power, *Yok*, a name which is affixed to any specific manifestation of it, and it is to this perception of feeling reduced to personality, that the 'Great Spirit' idea seems usually to have affixed itself.

The religious faith of the Dakotas is not in their gods as such. It is in a mysterious and intangible something of which they are only the embodiment . . . Each one will worship some of these divinities and neglect and despise others; but the great object of all their worship, whatever its chosen medium, is the *Taku Wakan*, which is the supernatural and mysterious. No one term can express the full meaning of the Dakota's *Wakan*. It comprehends all mystery, secret power and divinity.

Thus a Dakota priest explained that the forms we see are not the real forms but only their *tonwapi*, i.e. the manifestation of the divine power which possesses them. For every object in the world has a spirit. That

Spirit is *Wakan* – the divine power which comes from *Wakan beings* that are greater than mankind, just as mankind is greater than the animals.

Christopher Dawson, *Progress and Religion*

Myth and Reality

On the archaic level of culture religion maintains the opening towards a superhuman world, the word of axiological values. These values are 'transcendent' in the sense that they are held to be revealed by divine beings or mythological ancestors. As we have seen these models are conveyed by myths. Myths are the most general and effective means of awakening and maintaining consciousness of another world, a beyond, whether it be the Divine world or the world of the ancestors. This 'other world' represents a superhuman transcendent place, the place of absolute realities. It is the experience of the sacred, that is, an encounter with a trans-human reality, which gives birth to the idea that something really exists, that hence there are absolute values capable of guiding man and giving a meaning to human existence. It is then, through the experience of the sacred that the idea of reality, truth and significance first dawn, to be later elaborated and systematized by metaphysical speculations.

Mircea Eliade, *Myth and Reality*

Mana

Mana is, for the Melanesians, that mysterious but active power which belongs to certain people, and generally to the souls of the dead and all spirits. The mighty act of cosmic creation was not possible except through the *Mana* of the divinity: the chief of the clan also possesses this *Mana* . . .

The Sioux call this force *Wakan*. It circulates everywhere in the cosmos but only manifests itself in certain extraordinary phenomena (as the sun, moon, thunder, wind, etc.) and in strong personalities (sorcerers, Christian missionaries, mythical beings). The Iroquois employ the term *Orenda* to designate the same notion; a tempest has *Orenda* in it. The *Orenda* of a bird difficult to catch is very subtle; an angry man is a prey to his *Orenda*. *Oki* among the Hurons, *Zemi* among the people of the Antilles, *Megbe* among the African Pygmies, all these terms express the notion of *Mana*.

Mircea Eliade, *Patterns in Comparative Religion*

The Supreme Being

Manifested in the sky (heaven)
'Where the sky (heaven) is, there is God.'

African Ewe

What is beyond all doubt is the quasi-universality of beliefs in a divine, celestial being, creator of the universe, and guaranteeing the fertility of the earth.

(Thanks to the rains which it sends.) Such Beings are endorsed with infinite prescience and wisdom: the moral law and the tribal ritual have been inaugurated by them during their brief stay on earth; they watch over the laws and the lightning strikes those who infringe them.

Ibid. p. 47

Symbolism

It is certain that everything that man has handled, felt, encountered or loved can become a hierophany. We know, for example, that as a whole the gestures, plays, dances, children's games, toys etc. have a religious origin: they have been at one time gestures, plays or objects of cult. We know, likewise, that instruments of music, architecture, means of transport (animals, carriages, boats etc.), began by being sacred objects of sacred actions. One may believe that there exists no animal or plant of any importance which has not shared in 'sacredness' in the course of history. We know in the same way that the trades, arts, industries, techniques, have a sacred origin or have been clothed in the course of time with the values of a cult. This list could be followed by daily actions (rising, walking, running), by different kinds of work (hunting, fishing, agriculture), by all physiological actions (feeding, sexual life), probably also by the essential words of language, and so on.

Mircea Eliade

Sacramentalism

In fact, one of the principal differences which separates the man of the archaic cultures from modern man resides primarily in the incapacity of the latter to live his organic life (in the first place his life of love and nutrition) as a sacrament ... These are nothing but physiological acts for the modern, whereas they are for the man of the archaic cultures, sacraments, ceremonies through which he is brought into communion with the power of life itself. We shall see later that the power and the life are only epiphanies of the ultimate reality; these elementary acts become for the primitive a rite which helps man to approach reality, to insert himself in being, delivering himself from the automations of becoming, of the profane, of nothing.

We shall have occasion to see that the rite consisting always in the repetition of an archetypal action accomplished in *illo tempore* (at the beginning of 'history') by the ancestors of the gods, an attempt is made to give 'being', by means of a hierophany, to the most banal and insignificant acts. The rite coincides by repetition with its archetype, profane time is abolished. We assist, so to speak, at the same act accomplished in *illo tempore*, at the moment of the dawn of the world. By transforming, consequently, all the physiological acts into ceremonies, archaic man tries to 'pass out', to project himself beyond time (becoming) into eternity.

Symbolism of Sky

The simple contemplation of the sky provides in the consciousness of primitive man a religious experience. Such an affirmation does not necessarily imply any form of 'naturism'. For the archaic mind Nature is never exclusively 'natural'. The expression 'simple contemplation of the vault of heaven' has an entirely different sense if we apply it to primitive man who is open to daily miracles with an intensity which it is difficult for us to imagine. Such a contemplation is equivalent to a revelation. The sky reveals itself for what it is in reality – infinite, transcendent. The vault of heaven is par excellence something wholly 'other' than the little world represented by man and his living space. The symbolism of transcendence is derived, we could say, from the simple recognition of its infinite height. 'The Most High' becomes quite naturally an attribute of the divinity. The upper regions inaccessible to man, the sphere of the stars, acquire the divine characteristics of the transcendent, of absolute reality, of perpetuity. Such regions are the abode of the gods; it is to them that certain privileged beings come by rites of heavenly ascension; there are raised according to certain religious conceptions, the souls of the dead.

All this is deduced from the simple contemplation of the sky; but it would be a grave error to consider such a deduction as a logical, rational operation. The transcendental category of 'height', of the supra-terrestrial, of the infinite, reveals itself to man as a whole, to his intelligence as to his soul. The symbolism is 'given' immediately to consciousness, that is to man who discovers himself as such, to man who takes cognizance of his position in the universe. The primordial discoveries are linked in such an organic fashion to the drama of his life that the same symbolism determines at once the activity of the subconscious as of the most noble expressions of his spiritual life.

Mircea Eliade, *Patterns in Comparative Religion*

Initiation

Thanks to initiation one is given knowledge of the true hierophany, of the mythical descent of the clan, of the corpus of moral and social laws, in a word of the situation of man in the universe. Initiation is also an act of knowledge and not only a ritual of regeneration. Knowledge, the global comprehension of the world, the deciphering the unity of the cosmos, the revelation of the final causes, which sustain existence, etc. – are rendered possible thanks to the contemplation of the sky, to the celestial hierophany and to the supreme heavenly divinities.

All the same, we should deceive ourselves greatly if we were to see in these acts and these reflections only simple rational preoccupations (as does, for example,

W. Schmidt). They constitute, on the contrary, the acts of integral man, who is not aware obviously of the obsession with causality, but knows above all – that is to say, finds himself directly inserted in the problem of existence. All these revelations of a metaphysical nature (the origin of the human race, sacred history, of the divinity and ancestors, metamorphoses, the meaning of symbols, secret names etc.) made within the setting of initiation, have not exclusively in view the satisfaction of the neophyte's thirst to know, but in the first place pursue the fortification of his existence as a whole, the promotion of the continuity of life, and of plenty, the assurance of a better lot after death, etc . . .

This initiation, let us repeat, assures the regeneration of the initiate, while revealing to him secrets of a metaphysical nature; it satisfies his desire for life, power and knowledge. It shows the close tie which exists between the theophany (since in the ritual initiation is revealed the true nature and the true name of the divinity), soteriology (since in however elementary a way initiation ensures the salvation of the neophyte) and metaphysic (the revelations which are made about the principle and origin of the universe, or the origin of the human race etc.). But at the centre of the secret ceremony is found the sky divinity, the same divinity which once made the Universe, which created man and descended to the earth to establish the worship and the rites of initiation.

Symbolism of Mountain

The mountain is nearest the sky and this invests it with a double sacredness: on the one hand it participates in the spatial symbolism of transcendence, and on the other hand it is the domain par excellence, of the atmospheric hierophanies and as such the abode of all gods. All mythologies have a sacred mountain, variations more or less illustrious of the Greek Olympus ... The symbolic and religious value of mountains are innumerable. The mountain is often considered as the point of meeting of heaven and earth: thus a 'centre', the point through which passes the axis of the world, a region saturated with the sacred, a place where the passage between the different cosmic zones can be realized. So, according to Mesopotamian belief the 'Mountain of the World' unites heaven and earth, and Mount Meru of Indian mythology stands at the middle of the world ...

The mountain by the fact that it is the point of meeting between heaven and earth is found at the 'centre of the world' and is certainly the most elevated point of the earth. That is why the consecrated places – holy places, temples, places, sacred towns – are assimilated to mountains and become themselves 'centres', that is to say are integrated in a magical way with the summit of the cosmic mountain. Mounts Tabor and Gerizim in Palestine were also 'centres' and Palestine, the 'holy land', being thus considered as the highest part of the world, was not reached by the deluge . . . For Christians Golgotha is found at the centre of the world, for it is the summit of the cosmic mountain and also the place where Adam was created and buried. And according to Islamic tradition the highest place on earth is the Ka'ata since 'the polar star proves that it is exactly below the centre of the sky'.

The 'Sacred Place'

The sacred place is a microcosm because it *repeats* the cosmic country, because it *reflects* the All. The altar and the temple (or the funeral monument or the palace) which are further transformations of the primitive 'sacred place', are themselves also microcosms, because they are *centres* of the world, because they are found at the very heart of the universe and constitute an *imago mundi*. The idea of 'centre' of absolute reality – absolute because a receptacle of the sacred – is implied by the most elementary conceptions of the 'sacred place', a conception to which, as we have already seen, the sacred tree is never lacking. The stone represents reality par excellence; indestructibility and duration: the tree with its periodic regeneration manifests the sacred power in the order of life. There where the waters come to complete this country they signify the latent powers, germs of life, purification. The 'microcosmic country' is reduced in time to one of its constitutive elements, the most important – to the tree or sacred pillar. It is a reduction by absorption. The tree ends by expressing in itself alone the Cosmos, by incorporating under a form apparently static, the energy force of the Cosmos, its life and its capacity for periodical renovation.

The Consecration of Space

Cosmogony is the exemplary type of all constructions. Every town, every new house, that is built has to imitate anew and in a certain sense to repeat the Creation of the World. In fact, every town, every dwelling is found at the 'centre of the universe', and on this account the construction was not possible except by means of the abolition of profane space and time and the instauration of the sacred space and time. In the same way, as the form is an *imago mundi*, the house is a microcosm. The threshold separates the two spaces: the hearth is assimilated to the centre of the world, the central pole of the dwelling of the primitive arctic and the North American peoples is assimilated to the cosmic axis. When the form of the dwelling varies and the house is replaced by the yurt, the mythico-religious function of the central pillar is assured by the opening at the top intended for the escape of the smoke. On the occasions of sacrifices a tree is brought in whose top goes up through this opening. The sacrificial tree with its seven branches signifies the seven celestial spheres. So on the one hand the house is a likeness of the Universe, on the other it is regarded as situated at the centre of the world, the opening for the smoke being opposite to the polar star. Every house by the paradox of the consecration of space and by the rite of construction is seen to be transformed into a 'centre'. In this way all houses – like all temples, palaces, cities – are found to be situated at one and the same point, the Centre of the Universe. It is a question, one must recognize, of a transcendent space, of a totally different structure from the profane, compatible with a multiplicity and even an infinity of 'centres'.

The Myth of the Eternal Return

Beliefs in a cyclic time, an eternal return in the periodic destruction of the Universe and of Humanity, preface to a New Universe and a new humanity 'regenerated', all these beliefs attest above all the desire and hope of a periodic regeneration of past time, of *history*. At bottom, the cycle in question is a Great Year, to use a term which is well-known in Greek-Oriental terminology, the Great Year begins with a Creation and ends with a Chaos, that is to say with a complete fusion of the elements. A cosmic cycle contains a Creation, an 'existence' (=history, fulfilment, degeneration) and a return to Chaos (ekpurosis, Ragnarok, pralaya, Atlantis, apocalypse). In respect to structure a Great Year is to 'the year' what the year is to the month or the day. But what interests us in this context is above all the hope of a total regeneration of time, evident in all the

13

myths and doctrines implying cosmic cycles: every cycle begins in an absolute manner because all the past and all history have been definitely abolished thanks to a lightning reintegration in the Chaos.

We come up against, then, in man on all levels, the same desire to abolish profane time and to live in sacred time. Better still, we find ourselves face to face with the desire to regenerate time in its totality, that is to be able to live – to live humanly, historically – in eternity, by transfiguration of time into an eternal 'now'. This nostalgia for eternity is in some sense symmetrical with the nostalgia for Paradise . . . To the desire to find oneself perpetually and spontaneously in a sacred space corresponds the desire to live perpetually, thanks to the repetition of archetypal gestures, in eternity. The repetitions of the archetypes shows the desire to realize an ideal form (archetype) under the very conditions of human existence, to find oneself in time without bearing its burden, that is to say without submitting to its irreversibility . . . In this sense the myths and the rites connected with sacred space and time can be reduced, it would seem, to so many nostalgic memories of a terrestrial Paradise, and a sort of 'experimental' eternity, to which man thinks that he can still claim to have access.

Mircea Eliade, *Patterns in Comparative Religion*

Primitive Religion

The Konde of Tanganyika believe in a Supreme Being, *Kyala* or *Lesa*, who, like all the Supreme Beings of the Africans, is endowed with all the majesty of a heavenly, creating, omnipotent and law-giving god. But *Lesa* does not only show himself by means of epiphanies of the sky: Anything great of its kind, such as a great ox or even a great he-goat, or any other impressive object, is called *Kyala*, by which it may be meant that God takes up his abode temporally in these things. When a great storm lashes the lake into fury, God is walking on the face of the waters; when the roar of the waterfall is louder than usual, it is the voice of God. The earthquake is caused by his mighty footstep, and the lightning is *lesa*, God coming down in anger. God sometimes also comes in the body of a lion or a snake, and it is in that form that he walks among men to behold their doing.

Mircea Eliade, *Patterns in Comparative Religion*

Religion of the Nuer and Akan Peoples

To Nuer God who created all things and is Lord of life and death, is a spirit as ubiquitous as the wind or air. He is essentially a Sky God but he is not removed from the earth. He is close to man and at the same time separated from him. He falls in the rain, flashes in the lightning, rumbles in the thunder, and when he shines in the new moon, Nuer rub their foreheads with ashes (an act of

15

dedication) and pray, 'Great Father, let us be at peace'. He is great father and ancestor who gave them their food and culture and ritual powers, and in whom they find explanation for all things. He has no fixed earthly abode or shrine or prophets, communication with him is by prayers and sacrifices. But although God (*Kwoth*) is, to borrow an Old Testament metaphor, the God of Heaven, he is nevertheless connected with man and society in many ways. The spirits of the air, which are also known as Kwoth, are connected with particular personalities and groups in the society, and are all manifestations or 'refractions' of God. And during invocations it is not only the God or spirit in the sky who is invoked but also the spirits of the air, spirits of persons killed by lightning, totemic spirits, nameless age-mate spirits, and even 'spirit of my community'.

To Nuer these are all spirits, for they are all like air. God, however, though partaking of the same nature as the others, is yet not a particular spirit of the air. Nuer know the difference very well: a spirit of the air, for instance, has prophets and votaries, exacts demands and visits men with misfortunes. Yet any sacrifice to any of these spirits is also a sacrifice to God. The difference to note here is that whereas the one is creator and father of all, and is transcendent over all social groups, and invoked in all exceptional human misfortunes like earthquakes, the many in their various ways are associated separately with individuals and groups . . .

For the Akan believe in a supreme, immortal God who created all things and in whom again all things are explained. He gives to every man before he appears on earth a bit of Himself, which goes back to Him on the death of its possessors. To the Akan, God is known by many attributes, among which are The Everlasting, The Creator, The Dependable One. 'No one shows God to the child', they say, 'for he is known instinctively to exist, though he has no priests and is not worshipped.'

Nana Kobina NKetsia IV, *Springs of Morality*, ed. John Todd

Primitive Man

The intelligence of primitive man is of the same nature as ours: it can even be keener in him than in some civilized men. But that with which we are here concerned is a question of the state, of the conditions of the use of the mind. The whole mental regime of primitive man is contained under the primacy of the imagination. With him the intelligence is altogether bound up with and subordinate to the imagination and the savage universe. Such a mental regime is a regime of experimental and lived connection with nature, of whose intensity and breadth we can only form a picture with difficulty.

Here is an inferior condition but one by no means to be scorned, it is a human state, but a state of the childhood of humanity: a fruitful state and a state through which it was necessary to pass. In this regime humanity enriched itself by many vital truths, of which perhaps a great number were lost when it passed on to an adult state: those truths were known by means of dream or of instinct and of living appreciation just as the light of the intelligence was diffused before becoming focused in stars and in solar systems which separate daylight from shadow.

. . . Whenever primitive man is dealing with the understanding of the immediate concrete, with the interpretation and the practical use of data of the senses, in short, with the world of animal experience, primitive man's imagination, infused with intelligence, displays qualities properly intellectual; qualities of observation and perspicacity, of discernment, reasoning, of grasping the real in accordance with its typical diversities, in accordance with its concrete guidelines and differences . . . but whenever he is dealing with the world of abstract thought and of intelligible linkages, with the immensity of that which is to be known beyond the experience of the immediate concrete . . . at that moment he makes his intelligence labour under the law of the internal senses and of their dream activity. And how should it be otherwise? Hence it comes about that his imagination, infused with intelligence, enters into a regime of thought dominated by the lived participation on which ethnologists with good reason insist . . .

In similar fashion the religion of primitive man . . . was in a state of magic. His myths have a character which is above all practical.

'There is no doubt about the reason why the meaning of the myths must remain secret, even if their text is known. To possess this meaning is not only knowledge, but confers a power, which is dissipated if the myths are profaned . . . This power alone permits the tribe to enter into communion with its ancestors of a mythical period, in some way to participate in them, to make actual their presence, to ensure that their action is renewed periodically . . .' (Levy-Bruhl)

Maritain, *Sign and Symbol*

II

THE WAY OF POETRY

By poetry I mean not the particular art which consists in writing verses, but a process at once more general and more primary: that intercommunion between the inner being of Beings and the inner being of the human Self which is a kind of divination (as we realized in ancient times; the Latin *vates* was both a poet and diviner). Poetry is in this sense the secret life of all the arts; another name for what Plato called *mousikè*.

I use the words intellect and reason as synonymous, in so far as they designate a single power or faculty in the human soul. But I want to emphasize from the start that the very words reason and intellect, when they are related to the spiritual energy which is poetry, must be understood in a much deeper and larger sense than usual. The intellect as well as the imagination is the core of poetry. But reason or intellect is not merely logical reason; it involves an exceedingly more profound – and more obscure – life which is revealed to us in proportion as we endeavour to penetrate the hidden recesses of poetic activity. In other words, poetry obliges us to consider the intellect in its secret wellsprings inside the human soul and as functioning in a non-rational (I do not say anti-rational) or non-logical way.

Reason does not only consist of its conscious logical tools and manifestations, nor does the will consist only of its deliberate conscious determinations. Far beneath the sunlit surface thronged with explicit concepts and judgments, words, and expressed resolutions or movements of the will, are the sources of knowledge and creativity, of love and suprasensuous desires, hidden in the primordial translucid light of the intimate vitality of the soul. Thus it is that we must recognize the existence of an unconscious or preconscious which pertains to the spiritual powers of the human soul and to the inner abyss of personal freedom, and of the personal thirst and striving for knowing and seeing, grasping and expressing: a spiritual or musical unconscious which is specifically different from the automatic or deaf unconscious.

On the one hand, in our intellect is fecundated the intelligible germ on which all the formation of ideas depends. And it draws from them, and produces within itself, through the most vital process, its own living fruits, its concepts and ideas. But it knows nothing either of these germs it receives within or of the very process through which it produces its concepts. Only the concepts are known . . .

On the other hand, and this is the fundamental point for me, we possess in ourselves the illuminating intellect, a spiritual sun ceaselessly radiating, which activates everything in intelligence and whose light causes all our ideas to arise in us and whose energy permeates every operation of our mind. And this primal source cannot be seen by us; it remains concealed in the unconscious of the spirit. Furthermore it illuminates with its spiritual light the images from which our concepts are drawn. And this very process of illumination is unknown to us, it takes place in the unconscious; and often these very images without which there is no thought remain also unconscious or scarcely perceived in the process, at least for the most part. Thus it is that we know (not always, to be sure!) what we are thinking, but we don't know how we are thinking; and that before being formed and expressed in concepts and judgments, intellectual knowledge is at first a beginning of insight, still unformulated, a kind of many-eyed cloud which is born from the light of the illuminating intellect on the world of images, and which is but a humble and trembling inchoation, yet invaluable, tending towards an intelligible content to be grasped.

At this point we see how essential to poetry is the subjectivity of the poet . . . I mean subjectivity in its deepest, ontologic sense, that is the substantial totality of the human person, a universe unto itself, which the spirituality of the soul makes capable of containing itself through its own immanent acts, and which, at the centre of all the subject knows as objects, grasps only itself as subject. In a similar way to that in which divine creation presupposes the knowledge God has of his own essence, poetic creation presupposes as a primary requirement, a grasping by the poet of his own subjectivity in order to create.

But the substance of man is obscure to himself. He knows not his soul except in the fluid multiplicity of passing phenomena which emerge from it and are more or less clearly attained by reflective consciousness, but only increase the enigma, and leave him more ignorant of the essence of his Self. Or if he knows it, it is formlessly, by feeling it as a kind of propitious and enveloping night. Melville, I think, was aware of that when he observed that 'No man can ever feel his own identity aright except his eyes be closed; as if darkness were the proper element of our own essences.' Subjectivity, *as subjectivity*, is inconceptualizable; is an unknowable abyss. How then can it be revealed to the poet?

The poet does not know himself in the light of his own essence. Since man perceives himself only through a repercussion of his knowledge of the world of things, and remains empty to himself if he does not fill himself with the universe, the poet knows himself only on condition that things resound in him, and that in him at a single wakening they and he come forth together out of sleep. In other words the primary requirement of poetry, which is the obscure knowing, by the poet, of his own subjectivity, is inseparable from, is one with

23

another requirement – the grasping, by the poet, of the objective reality of the outer and inner world; not by means of concepts and conceptual knowledge, but by means of an obscure knowledge which I shall describe as knowledge through effective union.

His intuition, the creative intuition, is an obscure grasping of his own Self and of things in a knowledge through union or through connaturality which is born in the spiritual unconscious, and which fructifies only in the work. So the germ of which I spoke and which is contained in the spiritual night of the free life of the intellect, tends from the very start to a kind of revelation – to the humble revelation virtually contained in a small lucid cloud of inescapable intuition, both of the Self of the poet and of some particular flash of reality in the God-made universe; a particular flash of reality bursting forth in its unforgettable individuality, but infinite in its meanings and echoing capacity.

Poetic intuition is directed towards concrete existence as connatural to the soul pierced by a given emotion; that is to say, each time toward some singular existent, towards some complex of concrete and individual reality, seized in the violence of its sudden self-assertion, and in the total unicity of its passage in time . . . But poetic intuition does not stop at this given existent; it goes beyond, and infinitely beyond. Precisely because it has no conceptualized object, it tends and extends to the infinite, it tends toward all the reality, the infinite reality, which is engaged in any single existing thing, either the secret properties of its being involved in its identity and existential relations with other things or the other realities, all the other aspects or fructifications of being scattered in the entire world, which have in themselves the wherewithal to found some ideal relation with this singular existent thing, and which it conveys to the mind by the very fact that it is grasped through its union with and resonance in subjectivity spiritually awakened.

Such is, I think, the thing grasped by poetic intuition: the singular existent which resounds in the subjectivity of the poet together with all the other realities which echo in this existent and which it conveys in the manner of a sign.

As concerns finally the work, it will also be indissoluble unity – as the poetic intuition from which it proceeds – both a revelation of the subjectivity of the poet and of the reality that poetic knowledge has caused him to perceive. Be it a painting or a poem, this work is a made object – in it alone does poetic intuition come to objectivization. And it must always preserve its own conscience and value as an *object*. But at the same time it is a sign – both a *direct sign* of the secrets perceived in things, of some irrecusable truth of nature or adventure caught in the great universe, and a *reversed* sign of the subjective universe of the poet, of his substantial Self obscurely revealed. Just as things grasped by poetic intuition abound in significance, just as being swarms with signs, so the work also will swarm with meanings, and will say more than it is and will deliver to the mind at one stroke the universe in a human countenance.

The work will make present to our eyes together with itself, something else, and still something else, and still something else indefinitely, in the infinite mirrors of analogy.

Maritain, *Creative Intuition in Art and Poetry*

Transformation

Transitoriness is everywhere plunging into a profound Being. And therefore all the forms of the here and now are not merely to be used in a time-limited way, but, so far as we can, installed within those superior significances in which we share. Nature, the things we move about among, and use, are provisional and perishable; but so long as we are here, they are our possession and our friendship, sharers in our trouble and gladness, just as they have been the confidants of our ancestors. Therefore not only must all that is here not be corrupted or degraded, but just because of that very provisionality they share with us, all these things should be comprehended by us in a most fervent understanding and transformed. Transformed? Yes, for our task is to stamp this provisional perishing earth into ourselves so deeply, so painfully and passionately, that its being may rise again invisibly in us. We are the bees of the invisible . . .

26

The Elegies show us at this work; this work of the continual conversion of the dear visible, and tangible into the invisible vibration and agitation of our own nature, which introduces new vibration numbers into the vibration spheres of the universe . . .

The earth has no other refuge except to become invisible: in us, who through one part of our nature have a share in the invisible, or at least share-certificates, and can increase out holding in invisibility during our being here – only in us can this intimate and enduring transformation of the visible into an invisible no longer dependent on visibility and tangibility be accomplished, since our destiny is continually growing at once more actual and invisible within us.

Rilke, *Duino Elegies*, App. IV

Poetry and Mysticism

We believe then that a certain degree of intelligibility and likewise a certain degree of obscurity is found in every true work of poetry. Intelligibility and obscurity mark the origin of the work which is conceived in those depths of the soul where intelligence and desire, intuition and sensibility, imagination and love have their common source. When it begins to emerge from this ground of generation and nourishment, the work makes its appeal, each time in a different way, to those powers of the soul which have each their own manner of attaining the real and of speaking it forth.

27

The source of poetry and of all creative intuition is in a certain experience which one can call a knowledge obscure and tasted, of a taste altogether spiritual, for in these depths all is spirit and life, and every poet knows that he penetrates them by the recollection of all his senses, however fugitive it may be, which is the first condition of poetic conception.

This recollection is a psychological phenomena analogically common to the poetic state and to mystical contemplation. So also is the obscure and tasted knowledge which accompanies it . . . But one must understand that the kind of obscure knowledge or affective experience which is that of poetry does not touch in the same manner as the obscure knowledge of mystical experience at the common source of all that exists . . . In the mystic experience the object touched is the uncreated abyss, God the saviour and giver of life, known obscurely as present and united to the soul of him who contemplates; whereas the obscure knowledge which is that of the poet, and which touches, as the object which it knows, the things and reality of the world rather than God himself, derives from a union of another order, more or less intense, with God the creator and organizer of nature . . .

The recollection which produces such an experience acts as a bath of refreshment, of rejuvenation and of purification for the spirit. Is this the principle of the catharsis of Aristotle? We cannot estimate the depth of the response which our faculties then enjoy. It is a

28

concentration of all the energies of the soul, but a peaceful concentration, which is restful and not based on any kind of tension; the soul enters into its rest, in this place of refreshment and peace superior to all emotion. It dies the 'death of the angels', but it is to live again in that state of exaltation and enthusiasm which is wrongly called inspiration, because the inspiration was already present in this state of response, where it passed unperceived. Now the spirit reinvigorated and vivified enters into a joyous activity, so easy that everything appears to be given at that moment and to come from outside. In reality, it was already there in the shade, hidden in the spirit and in the blood; all that was to be put into the work was there, but we did not know it. We did not know how to discover it or to make use of it before we were steeped in the tranquil depth.

Raissa Maritain

The poet's intuition, creative intuition or emotion, is an obscure grasp of the self and of things together in a knowledge by union or connaturality, which is formed and bears fruit and has its 'word' only in the work, and which with all its vital weight bears on making and producing. This is a kind of knowledge which is very different from what one ordinarily calls knowledge, a knowledge which cannot be expressed in ideas and in judgments, but which is rather experience than knowledge, a creative experience which desires to express itself and can only be expressed in a work . . .

In short it is towards the totality of his being that the poet is brought, if he is docile to the gift which he has received, and consents to enter into the depths and allow himself to be stripped. We think that this poetry of integrity, of rather integration, not by an effort of voluntary concentration, but by the quietude of creative recollection and of poetic knowledge left to its true nature – is that which the actual situation of poetry authorizes us to hope for.

Jacques Maritain

It is then at the moment when it falls thus into these living sources that the emotion becomes intentional and intuitive, and passes into the condition of a grasp of the real; . . . not that it serves to objectify a term which specifies knowledge, but because it is itself taken up into the undetermined vitality and the productivity of the spirit, to which it brings a determination as a kind of germ. In it and in an inseparable way there then coexist the real and the self, the world and the whole soul. Then sense and sensation are taken up into the heart, the blood to the spirit, passion to intuition. And along with the vital actuation of the intellect, all the faculties are actuated likewise, in their depths and in their roots. It is the soul which is known in the experience of the world, and the world which is known in the experience of the soul . . .

Jacques Maritain

Poetic Knowledge

Poetry is produced not only by the mere caprice of pleasure but by natural necessity. It is so far from being superfluous and capable of elimination, that without it thought cannot arise: it is the primary activity of the human mind. Man before he has arrived at the stage of forming universals forms imaginary ideas. Before he reflects with a clear mind, he apprehends with faculties confused and disturbed: before he can articulate, he sings: before speaking in prose, he speaks in verse: before using technical terms, he uses metaphors, and the metaphorical use of words is as natural to him as that which we call natural.

Giambattista Vico, *Scienza Nuova*

D. H. Lawrence, *Apocalypse*

We have not the faintest conception of the vast range that was covered by the ancient sense-consciousness. We have lost almost entirely the great and intrinsically developed sensual awareness or sense awareness and sense-knowledge of the ancients. It was a great depth of knowledge arrived at directly by instinct and intuition, as we say, not by reason. It was a knowledge based not on words but on images. The abstraction was not into generalizations or into qualities but into symbols. And the connection was not logical but emotional. The now 'therefore' did not exist. Images or symbols succeeded

31

one another in a procession of instinctive and arbitrary physical connection – some of the Psalms give us examples – and they get nowhere because there was nowhere to get to; the desire was to achieve a certain consummation of a certain state of consciousness, to fulfil a certain state of feeling-awareness . . .

While men still thought of the heart or liver as the seat of consciousness, they had no idea of this 'on and on' process of thought. To them a thought was a completed state of feeling-awareness, a cumulative thing, a deepening thing, in which feeling deepened into feeling in consciousness, until there was a feeling of fulness. A completed thought was like the plumbing of a depth, like a whirlpool, or emotional awareness, and at the depth of this whirlpool of emotion, the resolve formed. But it was no stage in a journey. There was no logical chain to be dragged further.

D. H. Lawrence

Does the body correspond so intimately with the spirit? she asked herself. And she knew with the clarity of ultimate knowledge, that the body is only one of the manifestations of the spirit. The transmutation of the integral spirit is the transmutation of the physical body as well, unless I set my will, unless I absolve myself from the rhythm of life, fix myself and remain static, cut off from living, absolved within my own will. But better die than live mechanically a life that is a repetition of repetitions. To die is to move on with the invisible. To die is also a joy, the joy of submitting to that which is greater than the known, namely the pure unknown. That is a joy. But to live mechanized and cut off within the motion of the will, to live as an entity absolved from the unknown, that is shameful and ignominious. There is no ignominy in death. There is complete ignominy in an unreplenished, mechanized life. Life indeed may be ignominious, shameful to the soul. But death is never a shame. Death itself, like the illimitable space, is beyond our sullying . . .

How beautiful, how grand, how perfect death was, how good to look forward to . . . Oh let us ask no question of it, what it is or is not. To know is human, and in death we do not know, we are not human. And the joy of this compensates for all the bitterness of knowledge and the sordidness of our humanity. In death, we shall not be human, and we shall not know. The promise of this is our heritage, we look forward like heirs to our majority.

D. H. Lawrence, *Women in Love*

Goethe

Perhaps there was still the possibility of another method, one which would not tackle nature merely by dissecting and particularizing, but show her at work and alive, manifesting herself in her wholeness in every single part of her being.

To recognize living forms as such, to see in their context their visible and tangible parts, to perceive them as manifestation of something within and thus to master them, to a certain extent, in their wholeness through a concrete vision . . .

What determines living form is its innermost nucleus: the external elements modify its external appearances.

Colours are the actions and sufferings of light.

Truth is a revelation emerging at the point where the inner world of man meets the external reality . . . It is a synthesis of world and mind, yielding the happiest assurance of the external harmony of existence.

All that is transient is but a symbol.

Everything that exists is an analogy of existence itself.

A man born and bred in the so-called exact sciences, on the height of his analytical reason, will not easily comprehend that there is something like an exact concrete imagination.

Beauty is the manifestation of secret laws of nature which were it not for their being revealed through beauty would have remained unknown for ever.

In a true symbol the particular represents the universal, not as a dream or shadow, but as the living and instantaneous revelation of the unfathomable.

Erich Keller, *The Disinherited Mind*

The true symbol is the representation of the general through the particular, not, however, as a dream or shadow, but as the revelation of the unfathomable in a moment of life.

There must have been a time when the religious, aesthetic and moral perceptions were one.

Ibid.

Nietzsche and Goethe

Such a mind having attained to real freedom, lives at the very centre of all things with a joyful and confident acceptance of fate, lives in the faith that only the particular in its separateness is objectionable, and that in the wholeness of life everything is affirmed in its holiness – he no longer denies.

In looking at objects of Nature . . . while I am thinking . . . I seem rather to be seeking, as it were asking for, a symbolic language for something with me, that already and for ever exists.

Ibid. p.109

Rilke's Mystical Experience

He remembered the hour in that other garden (Capri) when, both outside and within him, the cry of a bird was correspondingly present, did not, so to speak, break upon the barriers of his body, but gathered inner and outer together into one uninterrupted space, in which mysteriously protected, only one single spot of purest, deepest consciousness remained. That time he had shut his eyes, so as not to be confused in so generous an experience by the contents of his body, and the infinite passed into him so intimately from every side that he could believe he felt the light responding of the already appearing stars within his breast.

Rilke, *Duino Elegies*, App. III

Carlyle

A musical thought is one spoken by a mind that has penetrated into the inmost heart of the thing; detected the inmost mystery of it, namely the *melody* that lies hidden in it; the inward harmony of coherence which is its soul, whereby it exists and has a right to be here in this world. All inmost things, we may say, are melodious; naturally utter themselves in song. The meaning of song goes deep. Who is there that in logical words can express the effect music has on us? A kind of inarticulate, unfathomable speech, which leads us to the edge of the infinite, and lets us for a moment gaze into that!

The Hero as Poet

All deep things are Song. It seems somehow the very central essence of us, Song; as if all the rest were but wrappages and hulls. The primal element of us; of us and all things. The Greeks talked of sphere-Harmonies: it was the feeling they had of the inner structure of

36

Nature; that the soul of all her voices and utterances was perfect music. Poetry therefore will call musical thought. The poet is he who *thinks* in that manner. At bottom it turns still on power of intellect; it is a man's sincerity and depth of vision that makes him a poet. See enough and you see musically; the heart of Nature being everywhere is music, if you can only reach it.

Ibid.

Good painting is nothing but a copy of the perfections of God and a recollection of His painting . . . It is a music and a melody which only intellect can understand, and that with great difficulty.

Michelangelo

From 'Lines written above Tintern Abbey'

Five years have passed; five summers, with the length
Of five long winters! and again I hear
These waters, rolling from their mountain-springs
With a soft inland murmur. Once again
Do I behold these steep and lofty cliffs,
That on a wild secluded scene impress
Thoughts of more deep seclusion; and connect
The landscape with the quiet of the sky . . .
         These beauteous forms
Through a long absence, have not been to me
As is a landscape to a blind man's eye:
But oft, in lonely rooms, and 'mid the din

Of towns and cities, I have owed to them,
In hours of weariness, sensations sweet,
Felt in the blood, and felt along the heart;
And passing even into my purer mind,
With tranquil restoration . . .
                    Nor less, I trust,
To them I may have owed another gift,
Of aspect more sublime; that blessed mood,
In which the burthen of the mystery,
In which the heavy and the weary weight
Of all this unintelligible world,
Is lightened: that serene and blessed mood,
In which the affections gently lead us on,
Until, the breath of this corporeal frame
And even the motion of our human blood
Almost suspended, we are laid asleep
In body, and become a living soul:
While with an eye made quiet by the power
Of harmony, and the deep power of joy,
We see into the life of things . . .
                    For I have learned
To look on nature, not as in the hour
Of thoughtless youth; but hearing oftentimes
The still, sad music of humanity,
Nor harsh nor grating, though of ample power
To chasten and subdue. And I have felt
A presence that disturbs me with the joy
Of elevated thoughts; a sense sublime

Of something far more deeply interfused,
Whose dwelling is the light of setting suns,
And the round ocean and the living air,
And the blue sky, and in the mind of man:
A motion and a spirit, that impels
All thinking things, all objects of all thought,
And rolls through all things. Therefore am I still
A lover of the meadows and the woods,
And mountains; and of all that we behold
From this green earth; of all the mighty world
Of eye, and ear, both what they half create,
And what perceive; well pleased to recognize
In nature and the language of the sense
The anchor of my purest thoughts, the nurse,
The guide, the guardian of my heart, and soul
Of all my moral being . . .

W. Wordsworth

THE WAY OF PHILOSOPHY

1 THE GREEK TRADITION

The Hermetic Mystery

As Agrippa moreover testifies, the soul of man, being estranged from the corporeal senses, adheres to a divine nature, from which it receives these things which it cannot search into by its own power: for when the mind is free, the reins of the body being loosed and going forth, as out of a closed prison, it transcends the bonds of the members, and nothing hindering, being stirred up in its proper essence, comprehends all things. And therefore man was said to be the express image of God, seeing he contains the Universal Reason within himself, and has a corporal similitude also with all, operation with all, and conversation with all. But he symbolizes with matter in a proper subject; with the elements in a fourfold body; with plants in a vegetable virtue; with animals in a sensitive faculty; with the heavens in an ethereal spirit and influx of the superior parts upon the inferior; with the angelical sphere in understanding and wisdom and with God in all. He is preserved with God and the intelligences by faith and wisdom; with celestial things by reason and discourse; with all inferior things by sense and dominion; and acts with all and has power on all, even on God himself, by knowing and loving Him. And as God knoweth all things, so man knowing Him can also know all things, seeing he has for an adequate object Being in general, or as some say, Truth itself: neither is there anything found in man, nor any disposition in which something of divinity may not shine forth; neither is there anything in God which may not also be represented in man. *Whosoever, therefore, shall know himself, shall know all things in himself*: but especially he shall know God, according to whose image he was made; he shall know the world, the resemblances of which he beareth, he shall know all creatures with which in essence he symbolizeth, and what comfort he can have and obtain from stones, plants, animals, elements; from spirits, angels, and everything: and how all things may be fitted for all things in their time, place, order, measure, proportion and harmony, even how he can draw and bring them to himself, as a loadstone, iron.

The Hermetic Mystery, ed. Atwood (pp. 148–9).

Man the Microcosm

Man, they say, is demonstrated to be a compendium of the whole created nature, and was generated to become wise and have a dominion over the whole of things; having within him besides those faculties, which he exerts ordinarily and by which he judges and contemplates sensible phenomena, *the germ of a higher faculty or Wisdom, which when revealed set alone, all the forms of things and hidden springs of nature become intuitively known and are implied essentially.* This Being, moreover, or faculty of Wisdom, is reputed to subsist with reference to nature as her substatal source, that it works magically withal, discovering latent properties as a principle, governing and supplying all dependent existence: and of this they speak magisterially, as if in alliance they had known the Omniscient Nature and in their own illumined understanding the structure of the universe.

(p. 164)

Wisdom

Thus strictly regarding the intellectual law as it proves and orders enquiry in common life, we have an image as it were an embryo conception of that archetypal wisdom, which the ancients celebrated as the occult essence of that law. And here we remark the grand divergence between modern and ancient metaphysics: that same law which the former recognizes as but an abstract boundary of thought only, having its object in sensibles, the latter proclaims absolutely to be the catholic subject of the great efficient force of nature, as known also and proved in the human conscience, when this is purified and passed back into contacting experience with its source. And this was Wisdom, Intellect, Divinization, *and the true man according to Plato and*

Aristotle is this Intellect; for the essence of everything is the summit of its nature.

(p. 167)

The Mystery of Existence

The greatest mystery of all is in Existence, and the only mystery; and as fire and light are one and everywhere perceived after the same manner, so is life in every particular the same inscrutable identity through all. Or does a vast and filled creation hang before our eyes and we think it to be without a foundation? Do we ourselves exist and consciously breathe, denying a mystery; or rather, admitting this, does anyone doubt that it is discoverable? Does not everything imply a necessary cause and is not each sustained still living in the same? And is it not absurd to suppose that we are entirely depending on externals, or that being in part self-dependent, we are so far depending on nothing? If, therefore, we contain within ourselves a proper principle of being, why should not this, thus proximate, be known? Behold, says the apostle, He is not far off from everyone of us; for 'in him we live, and move, and have our being' (Acts 17:28).

(p. 160)

Intuition and Reason

For we may observe that the evidence of reason even in common life, is irresistible, or more exactly to speak,

intuition is the evidence and end of every rational proof.
We believe in the phenomenon of existence spontaneously, but in the power of antecedents to produce their effects necessarily; in the idea of time, eternity is implied; with bound, infinity; as the unit is included in each dependent of a numerical series, and the mathematics have their evidence in intellectual assent: nor do we ever question the validity of the law, which thus abstractedly concludes within us, though our inferences from external facts are for ever varying and perpetually at fault.

(p. 165)

Wisdom in Aristotle

Thus Aristotle, for first example, since he will not be rated altogether as an enthusiast, in the beginning of his metaphysics declares Wisdom to be the highest science; adding that the wise man possesses a science of all things in intellect; not indeed derived from sensible particulars, but according to that which is universal and absolute in himself. In the Nicomachean Ethics, too, after showing intellect to be that power of the soul by which we know and prove things demonstratively, he further distinguishes Wisdom as the true being of that intellect; the science and intellection of things most honourable by nature; that though this part is small in bulk, yet it abounds in energy, and as much exceeds the composite nature of man in power, as in this energy which is the most delectable of all energies. And

44

throughout the Metaphysics, but more especially in the Twelfth Book, he demonstrates the necessary subsistence of incorporeal (ie. essential) being, and its efficacy in operation, when by the help of certain mystical exercises and preparations, the human understanding medium is made to pass into contact with its antecedent cause; that then it becomes to be a life in energy, and enjoys the most exalted and excellent faculty of discernment which was before occult, and the knowledge of which is inexpressibly blessed, and not to be conceived of by such as are not duly initiated and capable of this deification. True intellect, he says, is that which is essentially the most essential of that which is most essential; and it becomes intelligible by contact and intellection; and *that* Intellect is the same with the intelligible, the understanding recipient of the intelligible essence. Which essence too is Wisdom and the faculty we are discussing.

(p.168)

Plato

But Plato yet more plainly declares that to know oneself is Wisdom and the highest virtue of the soul; for the soul rightly entering into herself will behold all other things, and Deity itself; as verging to her own union and to the centre of all life, laying aside multitude and the variety of all manifold powers which she contains, she ascends to the highest watchtower of beings. According to Socrates, also, in the *Republic,* we read that Wisdom is generative of truth and intellect; and in the *Theaetetus* Wisdom is defined to be that which gives perfection to things imperfect and calls forth the latent intellections of the soul – and again, by Diotima in the *Banquet,* that mind which is become wise needs not to investigate any further, (since it possesses the true Intelligible); that is to say the proper object of intellectual inquiry in itself; and hence the doctrine of wisdom according to Plato may be sufficiently obvious.

(p.169)

Universals

As a rational promise to this life of a higher reality, the subsistence of these Universals cannot be too often or too distinctly brought to mind; for not only do they reveal in us a necessity of Being beyond present experience and understanding, but adumbrating, as it were, their antecedent light, assist much, if perspicuously beheld, to introduce the idea of that consummate Wisdom, *wherein this reason, becoming passive, receives the substance of her whole.*

Intellectual Vision

There are three modes of human vision recorded by St Augustine; the first external and belongs to the outward eye; the second that of imagination, by which representations are visible to the internal sense; the third is amagogie, and an intellectual sight drawn above, by which intelligible species are beheld, as a pure infusion of light to the understanding. The first mode is familiar; the second has already been discussed; but this third vision of the light is in Elysium: where the eye of the mind, no longer as heretofore looking from without inwardly, beholds its object through the atmosphere of the natural life; but contrariwise, having passed through this purifying to the centre is converted and raised, and as a unit now regards the circumference transitively, to the focus of her light. Porphyry beautifully likens this mode of being to a fountain, not flowing outwardly, but circularly scattering its stream into itself. And thus there is an assimilation established, as near as may be in consciousness, of the self-knowing and the self-known, yet with this motion of the soul, time is consubsistent, as changing her conceptions, she passes from one to another according to the self motion of her essence, and through her eyes being directed to the different forms which she contains, and which have the relation of parts to her whole essence; but eternity is consubsistent only with the permanence of intellect in itself. And thus though there is a grade above, yet this is the intellection of Elysium, *where the exemplary image of the Universal Nature is revealed.*

(pp. 237–8)

Sophocles

Oh that my lot may lead me in the path of holy inno-
cence of word and deed, that path which august laws
ordain, laws that in the highest empyrean had their
birth, of which heaven is the father alone, neither did
the race of mortal man beget them, nor shall oblivion
ever put them to sleep. The power of God is mighty in
them and groweth not old.

Oedipus Tyrannus

Plato

The nature of the living being was eternal. This quality
it was impossible to attach to the created universe. So
He thought to make a sort of *moving image of eternity*.
In constructing heaven, simultaneously he made an
image of eternity which continues always as a unity, an
image eternal by numerical process, namely that which
we have called time. For days and nights and months
and years did not exist before heaven came into existence; but at the moment when it came into existence he
devised their origin. All these parts of time: 'was' and
'will be' are aspects of time, and we are wrong in inad-
vertently applying them to universal essence. We say 'it
was', 'it is', 'it will be', but 'it is' is the only expression
properly applicable to essence, while 'it was' and 'it will
be' are properly said of the process which is in time. For
these are motions but that which is for ever immovably

the same cannot become either older or younger in time; it cannot be said that it once came into existence, or that it has now come into existence, or that it will be in future . . . These are aspects of time which imitates eternity and moves in a numerical cycle.

(*Timaeus* 37D–38A)

Plato

What we shall see is something like a battle of gods and giants going on between them over their quarrel about reality. One party is trying to drag down everything to earth, out of heaven and the unseen, literally grasping rocks and trees in their hands for they lay hold upon every rock and stone and strenuously affirm that real existence belongs only to that which can be handled and offers resistance to the touch. They define reality as the same thing as body, and as soon as one of the opposite party asserts that anything without a body is real, they are utterly contemptuous and will not listen to another word. Accordingly their adversaries are very wary in defending their position somewhere in the heights of the unseen, maintaining with all their force that true reality consists in certain intelligible and bodiless forms. In the course of argument they shatter and pulverize those bodies which their opponents wield, and what others allege to be true reality, they call not real being but a certain moving process of becoming.

The Sophist – (from *Plato's Theory of Knowledge*,
by F. M. Cornford)

Plato

The idea of the first good simply cannot be expressed in
words, but when man has long been familiar with that
good, a light suddenly appears and blazes out in his
soul, as if it had flashed from a fire.

(7th letter)

Plato

The soul when using the body as an instrument of
perception, that is to say when using the sense of sight
or hearing or any other sense ... is then dragged by the
body into the region of the changeable, and wanders
and is confused. But when returning into herself she
reflects, then she passes into the other world, the region
of purity and eternity, and immortality and unchange-
ableness, which are her kindred, and with them she ever
lives when she is by herself and is not let or hindered;
then she ceases erring and being in communion with the
unchanging and invariable. And this state of the soul is
called wisdom.

Phaedo

Plato's Doctrine of Anomnesis

The soul of man is immortal and at one time reaches an

end which is called 'dying', and is 'born again' but is never slain.

(Meno 81 B)

The soul of us existed before we were born.

(Phaedo 77 A)

Admonishing the soul to collect and assemble herself in her self, and to trust in nothing but her self, that she may know her self itself, the self of (all) beings.

(Phaedo 83 B)

That teaching whereby what has not been heard is heard, what has not been thought is thought, what has not been known is known, just as by one piece of clay everything that is made of clay may be known...

(Timaeus 50 A,B)

Plotinus – The Archetypal World

Admiring the world of sense as we look out upon its vastness and beauty and the order of its eternal march, thinking of the gods within it, seen and hidden, and the celestial spirits and all the life of animal and plant, let us mount to its archetype, to the yet more authentic sphere: there we are to contemplate all things as members of the intellectual – eternal in their own right, vested with a self-springing consciousness and life, and presiding over all these, the unsoiled intelligence and the unapproachable wisdom.

The archetypal world is the true Golden Age, the age of Kronos, who is the Intellectual-Principle as being the offspring or exuberance of God. For here is contained all that is immortal: nothing here but is divine mind: all is God: this is the place of every soul. Here is rest unbroken: for how can that seek change in which all is well; what need that reach to, which holds all within itself: what increase can that desire which stands utterly achieved? All is content, thus, is perfect, that itself may be perfect throughout, as holding nothing that is less than divine, nothing that is less than intellective. Its knowing is not by search but by possession, its blessedness inherent not acquired; for all belongs to it eternally and it holds the authentic eternity initiated by Time, which circling round the soul, makes towards the new thing, passing the old. Soul deals with thing after thing – now Socrates, now a horse; always some one entity from among beings – but the Intellectual-Principle is all and *therefore its entire content is simultaneously present in that identity*; this is pure being in eternal actuality: nowhere is there any future for every then is a now; nor is there any past, for nothing there has ever ceased to be; everything has taken its stand forever, an identity well-pleased, we might say, to be as it is; and everything in that entire content is Intellectual-Principle and Authentic Existence; and the total of all is Intellectual Principle entire and Being entire.

Enneads V. i. 4.

The Knowledge of the Self

Thus the self-knower is a double person: there is the one
that takes cognizance of the principle in virtue of which
understanding occurs in the soul or mind; and there is
the higher knowing himself by the Intellectual-Principle
with which he becomes identical; and this latter knows
the self as no longer man but as a being that has become
something other through and through: he has thrown
himself as one thing over into the superior order, taking
with him only that better part of the soul, which alone is
winged for the intellectual act and gives the man once
established there the power to appropriate what he has
seen.

We can scarcely suppose this understanding faculty
to be unaware that it has understanding; that it takes
cognizance of things external; that in its judgments it
decides by the rules and standards within itself held
directly by the intellectual principle: that there is something higher than itself, something moreover which has
no need to seek but fully possesses. What can we
conceive to escape the self-knowledge of a principle
which admittedly knows the place it holds and the work
it has to do? It affirms that it springs from the
Intellectual-Principle whose second and image it is, that
it holds within itself all the universe of things, engraved
so to say, upon it as all is held there by the eternal
engraver. Aware so far of itself, can it be supposed to

halt at that? Are we to suppose that all we can do is to apply a distinct power of our nature and come thus to awareness of the Intellectual-Principle as aware of itself? Or may we not appropriate that principle – which belongs to us as we to it – and thus attain to awareness both of it and of ourselves? Yes: this is the necessary way we are to experience the self-knowledge vested in the Intellectual-Principle. And a human becomes Intellectual-Principle when ignoring all other phases of his being, he sees through that only and sees only that and so knows himself by means of the self, in other words attains the Self-Knowledge which the Intellectual-Principle possesses.

Enneads V. iii. 4.

Knowledge of the Supreme

All the need is met by a contact purely intellective. At the moment of touch there is no power whatever to make any affirmation; there is no leisure; reasoning upon the vision is for afterwards. We may know we have had the vision when the soul has suddenly taken light. This light is from the Supreme and is the Supreme; we may believe in the presence when, like that other god on the call of a certain man, He comes bringing light. The light is the proof of the advent: Thus the soul unlit remains without that vision: lit, it possesses what it sought. And this is the true end set before the soul, to take that light, *to see the Supreme by the Supreme and not by the light of any other principle* – to see the Supreme which is also the means to the vision; for that which illumines the soul is that which it is to see, just as it is by the sun's own light that we see the sun.

Enneads V. iii. 17.

This Principle of which the sun is an image, where has it its dawning, what horizon does it surmount to appear?

It stands immediately above the contemplating intellect which has held itself at rest towards the vision, looking to nothing else but the good and beautiful, setting its entire being to that in a perfect surrender, and now tranquilly filled with power and taking a new beauty to itself, gleaming in the light of that presence.

This advent, still, is not by expectation: it is a coming without approach: the vision is not of something that must enter but of something present before all else, before the intellect itself made any movement. Yet it is the intellect that must move, to come and to go, going because it has not known where it should stay and where that presence stays, the nowhere contained.

And if the intellect too could hold itself in that nowhere – not that it is ever in place, it too is uncontained, utterly unplaced – it would remain for ever in the vision of its prior, *or rather not in vision but in identity, all duality annulled.*

Enneads V. v. 8.

2 THE CHINESE TRADITION

Chuang-Tzu

Do not inquire whether the Tao is in this or in that: It is in all beings. That is why it is given the epithet of great, supreme, entire, universal, total . . . That which caused beings to be being is not Itself subject to the same law as beings. That which caused all beings to be limited is Itself limitless, infinite . . .

As for manifestation the Tao produces the succession of its phases but is not that succession. It is the author of condensations and dissipations but is not Itself condensation or dissipation. Everything proceeds from It and is modified by It and under Its influence. It is in all beings by the determining of a norm, but It is not Itself identical with beings, being neither differentiated nor limited.

O Tao, Thou who bestowest on all beings that which befits them, Thou hast never claimed to be equitable. Thou whose benefits extend to all times, Thou hast never claimed to be called charitable. Thou who was before the beginning and who dost not claim to be called venerable, Thou who enfoldest the universe and supportest it, producing all forms without claiming to be called skilful; it is in Thee that I move.

It can be said of the Tao only that it is the origin of everything and that it influences all while remaining indifferent.

The Tao, indifferent, impartial, lets all things follow their course without influencing them. It claims no title. It acts not. Doing nothing, there is nothing it does not do.

Not to know it is to know it; to know it is not to know it. But how is one to understand this, that it is by not knowing it that it is known? This is the way, says the Primordial State. The Tao cannot be heard; that which is heard is not It. The Tao cannot be seen; that which is seen is not It. The Tao cannot be uttered; that which is uttered is not It . . . The Tao not being imaginable, is not to be described. Whoever asks questions about the Tao and whoever answers them, both show that they do not know what the Tao is. Concerning the Tao one can neither ask nor make answer what It is.

All is one: during sleep the undistracted soul is absorbed into this Unity; in the waking state being distracted it distinguishes diverse beings.

It (the being which is united with the Tao) will no longer be dependent on anything; it will be perfectly free . . . It is also most justly said; the superhuman being has no longer an individuality of its own; the transcendent man has no longer any action of his own; the Sage has not even a name of his own; for he is one with the All.

Translated by Fr Weiger
quoted by R. Guenon – *Man and His Becoming*

Chuang-Tzu

Knowledge of the great One, of the great Negative, of the great Name, of the great Uniformity, of the great Space, of the great Truth, of the great Law – this is perfection. The great One is omnipresent. The great Negative is omnipotent. The great Name is all-inclusive. The great Space is all-assimilative. The great Truth is all-exacting. The great law is all-binding.

The ultimate end is heaven (tien). It is manifested in the laws of nature. It is the hidden spring. It was in the beginning.

This however is inexplicable. It is unknowable. But from the unknowable we reach the known.

Translated by H. A. Giles, quoted in *One in All*, p. 97

3 THE BUDDHIST TRADITION

Edicts of King Ashoka

Happiness in this world and in the next is difficult to secure without an extreme zeal for religion (dharma), a rigorous supervision, a perfect obedience, a lively sense of responsibility, and a constant activity. But thanks to my instruction this anxiety and zeal for dharma increase and will increase day by day . . . For the rule is this: government by dharma, law by dharma, security by dharma.

Edict 1

But it will be asked, What is this dharma? Dharma consists in doing the least possible evil and the greatest possible good – in mercy, charity, truth, and purity of life . . .

Edict II

One sees only his good acts and says, I have done such a good act. But one does not see his evil acts, and does not say, I have committed this evil act: this act is a sin. Such examination is painful, it is true, but nevertheless, it is necessary to question oneself, such things are sinful as mischief, cruelty, anger and pride. It is necessary to examine oneself. Carefully say, I will not harbour envy nor calumniate others. This will be beneficial to me here below; this will be in truth still more beneficial to me in the life to come.

Edict III

I have reflected that kings in times past desired that men should make progress in dharma, and men make no progress in dharma, according to their desire. By what means can I lead them in the right path? By what means can I cause them to make progress in dharma according to my desire? By what means can I cause them to advance in dharma? Then thus spoke King Priyadasi (Ashoka) beloved of the gods. I have formed the resolution of publishing religious exhortations, of promulgating religious instructions, so that men on hearing these will enter on the right paths, and will elevate themselves.

Edict VII

In this way acts of dharma are promoted in the world as well as the practice of dharma – via mercy and charity, truth and purity, kindness and goodness.

Edict VIII

Mahayana Doctrine

If the son or daughter of a family wishes to perform the study in the deep Perfect Wisdom, he must think thus:

There are five skandhas, and these must be considered as by their nature empty (void). Form is emptiness, and emptiness is form. Emptiness is not different from form, and form is not different from emptiness. What is form, that is emptiness, what is emptiness, that is form. Thus perception, name, conception and knowledge also are emptiness. Thus, O Sariputra, all things have the character of emptiness, they have no beginning and no end, they are faultless and not faultless, they are not imperfect, not perfect. Therefore, O Sariputra, here in this emptiness, there is no form, no perception, no name, no concept, no knowledge. No eye, ear, nose, tongue, body and mind. No form, sound, smell, taste, touch and objects. There is no eye (etc. till we come to) no mind, no objects, no mind knowledge. There is no knowledge, no ignorance, no destruction (of ignorance), there is no decay and death, no destruction of decay and death; there are not (The Four Truths) that there is pain, origin of pain, stoppage of pain and the way to it. There is no knowledge, no obtaining, no not-obtaining of Nirvana. Therefore, O Sariputra, there is no obtaining of Nirvana. A man who has approached the Perfect Wisdom of the Bodhisattvas dwells (for a time) enveloped in consciousness. But when the envelopment of consciousness has been annihilated, then he becomes free of all fear, beyond the reach of change, enjoying final Nirvana.

Therefore we ought to know the great verse of the Prajnaparamita, the verse of the great wisdom, the unsurpassed verse, the verse which appeases all pain – the verse proclaimed in the Prajnaparamita:

O WISDOM, GONE, GONE, GONE, TO THE OTHER SHORE, LANDED AT THE OTHER SHORE, SVAHA.

(From the larger *Prajnaparamitahridayasutra*)

Gate, gate, paragate,
parasamgate, bodhi svaha!
Gone, gone, gone beyond,
Gone altogether beyond,
O, What an awakening,
All Hail!

Mahayana

When appearances and names are put away and all discrimination ceases, that which remains is the true and essential nature of things, and as nothing can be predicated as to the nature of essence, it is called Suchness (Ta tha ta) of Reality. This universal, indifferentiated, inscrutable Suchness is the only Reality but it is variously called Reality (Dharma), Body of Reality (Dharma-Kaya), Noble Knowledge (Arya-Jnana), Noble Wisdom (Arya-Prajna). This Dharma of the imagelessness of the Body of reality is the Dharma which has been proclaimed by all the Buddhas, and when all things are understood in full agreement with it, one is in possession of Perfect Knowledge (Prajna) and is on the way to the attainment of the Noble Knowledge of the Tathagatas.

There has always been an eternally abiding reality. The realm of Reality (dharma-dhatu) abides for ever whether a Tathagata (one who has Thus-come) appears in the world or not. So does the Realness of all things (dharmata) eternally abide: so does the Supreme (Paramartha) abide and keeps its order. What has been realized by myself and all the Tathagatas is this Body of Reality (dharma-kaya), the eternally abiding, self-orderliness of Reality: the suchness (tathata) of things, the realness (bhutata) of things: Noble Wisdom which is Truth Itself. The Sun radiates its splendour on all alike: in like manner do the Tathagatas radiate the Truth of Noble Wisdom with no recourse to words and to all alike.

From the *Lankavatara Sutra*

Mahayana Doctrine

I make my obeisance to the Buddha who is wise, free from all attachment, and whose powers are beyond conception, and who has kindly taught the truth which cannot be expressed in words.

In the transcendental truth there is no origination, and in fact there is no destruction. The Buddha is like the sky (which has neither origination nor cessation) and the beings are like him, and therefore they are of the same nature.

There is no birth either on this side or on that. A compound thing originates from its conditions: therefore it is void by nature: this fact comes into the range of knowledge of one who knows all.

All things by nature are regarded as reflections. They are pure and naturally quiescent, devoid of any duality, equal, and remain always and in all circumstances thus (tathata).

In fact, worldlings attribute atman to what is not atman and in the same way they imagine happiness, misery, indifference, passions and liberation.

Birth in the six realms of existence in the world, highest happiness in heaven, great pain in hell, these do not come within the purview of truth; nor do the notions that unmeritorious actions lead to extreme misery, old age, disease and death, and meritorious actions surely bring about good results.

As a painter is frightened by the terrible figure of a Yaksa he has drawn, so is a fool frightened in the world (by his own false notions).

Even as a fool going himself into a quagmire is drowned therein, so are beings drowned in the quagmire of false notions and are unable to come out thereof. The feeling of misery is experienced by imagining a thing which in fact has no existence. Beings are tortured by the poison of false notions regarding the object and its knowledge.

Seeing these helpless beings with a compassionate heart one should perform the practices of the highest knowledge (bodhicarya) for the benefit of them.

Having acquired requisites thereby and getting unsurpassable bodhi, one should become a Buddha, the friend of the world, being freed from the bondage of false notions.

He who realizes the transcendental truth knowing the pratityasamutpada (ie. the manifestation of entities depending on their causes and conditions) knows the world to be void (sunya) and devoid of beginning, middle and end.

The samsara and nirvana are mere appearances: the truth is stainless, changeless, and quiescent from the beginning illumined.

The object of knowledge in dreams is not seen when one awakes. Similarly the world disappears to him who is awakened from the darkness of ignorance.

One having origination does not originate himself. Origination is a false conception of the people. Such conceptions and beings are not reasonable.

All this is nothing but mind (citta) and exists just like an illusion. Hence originate good and evil actions and from them good and evil birth.

When the wheel of the mind is suppressed, all things are suppressed. Therefore all things are devoid of atman and consequently they are pure.

It is due to thinking things which have no independent existence as eternal, atman, and pleasant that this ocean of existence (bhava) appears to one who is enveloped by the darkness of attachment and ignorance.

Who can reach the other side of the great ocean of samsara which is full of the water of false notions without getting into the great vehicle (mahayana)?

From the *Mahayanavimsaka* of Nagarjuna

4 THE HINDU TRADITION

When I was at sea last August, on my voyage to this country which I had long and ardently desired to visit, I found one evening, on inspecting the observations of the day, that India lay before us, and Persia on our left, whilst a breeze from Arabia blew nearly on our stern. A situation so pleasing in itself, and to me so new, could not fail to awaken a train of reflections in a mind which had early been accustomed to contemplate with delight the eventful histories and agreeable fictions of the eastern world. It gave me inexpressible pleasure to find myself in the midst of so noble an amphitheatre, almost encircled by the vast regions of Asia, which has ever been esteemed the nurse of sciences, the inventress of delightful and useful arts, the scene of glorious actions, fertile in the productions of human genius, abounding in natural wonders, and infinitely diversified in the forms of religion and government, in the laws and manners, customs and languages, as well as in the features and complexions of men.

Sir William Jones, First Discourse

To instruct others is the prescribed duty of learned Brahmans, and if they be men of substance, without reward; but they would all be flattered with an honorary distinction: and the Mahemedans have not only the permission but the positive command of their law giver, to search for learning even in the remotest parts of the globe.

Second Discourse

The inhabitants of the extensive land are described by Mr Lord with great exactness and with a picturesque elegance peculiar to our ancient language: 'A people', says he, 'presented themselves to mine eyes, clothed in linen garments somewhat low descending, or a gesture and garb, as I may say, maidenly and well-nigh effeminate, or a countenance shy and somewhat extranged, yet smiling out a glossed and bashful familiarity'.

On the Hindus

The Sanskrit language, whatever be its antiquity, is of a wonderful structure, more perfect than the Greek, more copious than the Latin and more exquisitely refined than either, yet bearing to both of them a stronger affinity both in the roots of verbs and forms of grammar, than could have possibly been produced by accident: so strong indeed that no philologer could examine them all three, without believing them to have sprung from some common source, which perhaps no longer exists; there is a similar reason, though not quite so forcible, for supposing that both the Greek and the Celtic, though blended with a different idiom, had the same origin with the Sanskrit; and the old Persian might be added to the same family, if this were the place for discussing any questions concerning the antiquities of Persia.

On the Hindus

We believe that it is our humble mission to preach and establish the principle of the unity of religions (as laid down by Keshava of the Brahmosamaj).

We mean to preach the reconciliation of all religions in Christ whom we believe to be perfectly divine and perfectly human.

The Blade, p. 39

By birth we are Hindus and shall remain Hindu till death. But as dvija (twice-born) by virtue of our sacramental rebirth, we are Catholic. We are members of an indefectible communion embracing all ages and climes.

In customs and manners, in observing caste and social destructions, in eating and drinking, in our life and living, we are genuine Hindus: but in our faith we are neither Hindu nor European nor American nor Chinese, but all inclusive. Our faith fills the whole world, and is not confined to any country or race; our faith is universal and consequently includes all truths.

Our thought and thinking is emphatically Hindu. We are more speculative than practical, more given to synthesis than analysis, more contemplative than active. It is extremely difficult for us to learn how to think like the Greeks of old or the scholastics of the Middle Ages. Our brains are moulded in the philosophic cast of our ancient country.

We are proud of the stability of the Hindu race. Many a mighty race did rise and fall, but we continue to exist, though we had to buffet many a religious deluge and weather many a political storm. We believe in the future greatness of our race and in this belief we shall live and die.

The more strictly we practise our universal faith, the better do we grow as Hindus. All that is noblest and best in the Hindu character is developed in us by the genial inspirations of the perfect Narahari – (God-man), our pattern and guide. The more we love Him, the more we love our country, the prouder we become of our past glory.

Do we really believe in Hinduism? The question must be understood, before it can be answered. Hinduism has no definite creed. Kapila and Vyasa were opposed to each other and yet both of them are considered to be rishis. The Hindu Vedantists of the school of Ramanuja look down upon the Hindu Vedantists of the school of Sankara as blasphemers; the Vaishnavu doctrines differ as widely as the poles from the Shaiva doctrine: even the gods have to fight one another in the Puranas. The test of being a Hindu cannot therefore be in religious opinions.

However, we are fully embued with the spirit of Hinduism. We hold with the Vedantists that there is one eternal essence from which proceed all things. We believe with the Vaishnavas in the necessity of incarnation and in the doctrine that man cannot be saved without grace. We agree in spirit with the Hindu lawgivers in regard to their teaching that sacramental rites (Samskaras) are vehicles of sanctification. With wondering reverence do we look on their idea of establishing a sacerdotal hierarchy vested with the highest religious authority in religious and social matters.

In short we are Hindus as far as our physical and mental constitution is concerned, but in regard to our immortal souls, we are Catholic. We are Hindu Catholics.

The Blade, pp. 71–3

India

My mind is in an ecstasy with the deep and grand unity which I have discovered running through all of India's various manifestations and her manifold strivings, and this prevents me from shrinking to stand in the dust with the poorest and most ignorant of my countrymen. This message of India some may understand, some may not – that makes no difference in my feeling that I am one with all India, that all her people are mine: and I have no doubt that through all of them the spirit of India is secretly and constantly working.

Rabindranath Tagore (Goa)

Vedanta (Avaita)

The knower of Brahman enjoys all desires, all delights procurable by desirable objects, without exception. Does he enjoy suns, heavens etc. alternately, as we do? No, he enjoys all desirable things simultaneously, as amassed together in a single moment, through a single perception, which is eternal like the light of the sun, which is non-different from the essence of Brahman, and which we have described as Reality, Knowledge, Infinite ... He enjoys all things by that Brahman whose nature is omniscience.

Sankara Taittiriya Upanishads Bhasya, 2.1.1.

Maya

An appearance of being, without origin, inexpressible in terms of being as of not being.

Anadir bhavarupa sadasadanirvacaniya

Sankara Brahma Sutra Bhasya

Lord, although I and Thou make but one, yet I (am related) belong to Thee and not Thou to me, just as the waves belong to the sea and not the sea to the waves.

Hymn to Hari

That which is the end of the agitation of the mind and supreme peace; that which is the Manikarnika and the supreme pilgrimage; that which is the primordial Ganges, the river of knowledge; that is Benares, the inborn wisdom, and that am I.

Sankara Kashipanchakam

This whole multiplicity of creatures existing under name and form in so far as it is Being itself is true: of itself it is untrue.

Com. on *Chandogya Upanishad* VI. iii. 2.

The Presence of God in his Image

God when present in the animate idol becomes in all respects subject to his devotee. Though omniscient, he seems to be without knowledge; though alive and conscious, he seems to be inanimate; though independent he seems to depend entirely on others; omnipotent, he seems to be powerless; though perfect, he appears needy; the protector of the universe appears helpless; he is the Lord, but he hides his Lordship; the invisible makes himself an object for our senses to perceive; the incomprehensible being brings himself within our easy reach; he makes himself present and near to us in holy places and shrines and temples, in our towns and villages, and in our very homes, and in the person of holy men.

from the *Artha Pancaka* of Pillai Lokacarya,
Thirteenth-Century Tamil

Visishtadvaita Vedanta

There is a highest Brahman which is the sole cause of the entire universe, which is antagonistic to all evil, whose essential nature is infinite knowledge and blessedness, which comprises within itself numberless auspicious qualities, of supreme excellence, which is different in nature from all other beings, and which constitutes the inner self of all. Of this Brahman the individual selves – whose true nature is unlimited knowledge and whose only essential attribute is the intuition of the Supreme Self – are modes in so far as they constitute its body. The true nature, however, of these selves is obscured by ignorance, that is the influence of the beginningless chain of works; and by release we have to understand that intuition of the highest Self, which is the natural state of the individual selves, and which follows on the destruction of ignorance . . .

Ramaniya Bhasya on *Vedanta Sutras*, 1. ii. 12

The cessation of such bondage is to be obtained only through the grace of the highest Self pleased by the devout meditation of the worshipper.

1. i. 1

The divine Supreme Person, all of whose wishes are eternally fulfilled, who is all-knowing and the ruler of all, whose every purpose is immediately fulfilled, having engaged in sport befitting his might and greatness, and having settled that work is of twofold nature, such and such works being good and such and such being evil, and having bestowed on all the individual selves, bodies and sense-organs, capacitating them for entering on such work and power of ruling those bodies and organs, and having himself entered into those selves as their inner Self, abides within them, controlling them as animating and cheering principle. The selves, on their side, endorsed with all the powers imparted to them by the Lord, and with bodies and organs bestowed by him, and forming abodes in which he dwells, apply themselves on their own part, and in accordance with their own wishes, to works either good or evil. The Lord then recognizing him who performs good actions as one who obeys his commands blesses him with piety, riches, worldly pleasure and final release.

1. ii. 12

The individual self is a part of the highest Self; as the light issuing from a luminous thing, such as fire or the sun, is part of the body; or as generic characteristics of a cow or a horse, and the white and black of things so coloured, are attributes and hence parts of the things in which these attributes adhere; or as the body is part of an embodied being. For by a part we understand that which constitutes one place (desa) of some thing, and hence a distinguishing attribute (visesana) is a part of the thing distinguished by that attribute . . . Now although the distinguishing attribute and the thing distinguished thereby stand to each other in the relation of part to whole, yet we observe them to differ in essential character. Hence there is no contradiction between the individual and the highest Self – the former of which is a distinguishing attribute of the latter standing in relation to each other as part to whole, and their being at the same time of essentially different nature.

II. iii. 45

Sivananda
OM

Adoration to the Supreme Being who dwells in the hearts of all beings, who is in the fire and the water, who is in the plants, herbs and trees, who is in the stone, brick and iron bars, and who has pervaded the whole universe.

I bow to the Secret of Secrets. I bow to Thee,

indweller of hearts. I bow to Thee, O Silent Witness of all activities of all minds. I bow to Thee, O inner Ruler of all beings, who pervades and permeates and interpenetrates things in this universe.

Salutation to Thee, Supreme Lord. Thou art without beginning and without end. Thou art the flower. Thou art the bee. Thou art woman. Thou art man. Thou art the sea, Thou art the waves. Thou art the old man tottering with a stick. Thou art the saint. Thou art the rogue.

Thou art Light divine. Thou art light of knowledge. Thou art dispeller of darkness. Thou art the Supreme Guru. Thou art beyond the reach of mind or speech. Thou art beyond any kind of limitation. Thou art the Over-Soul. Thou art the Self of the Universe.

Thou art Self-luminous. Thou art without parts, without actions, without limits, without any taint of fault, without birth and death. Thou art our Father, Mother, friend, relative, guru and sole refuge. Thou art the embodiment of peace, bliss, knowledge, power, strength and beauty.

O all merciful Lord, through grace may I realize Truth. May I always entertain sublime thoughts. May I realize myself as the light divine. May I serve humanity with atma bhava. May I be free from greed, lust, egoism, jealousy, hatred. May I behold the one, sweet, immortal Self in all beings. May I realize Brahman with pure understanding.

May the Light of lights ever guide me. May he

cleanse my mind of all impurities. May he inspire me. May he bestow on me power, courage and strength. May he remove the veil from my mind. May he remove all obstacles in the spiritual path. May he make my life happy and fruitful.

I bow to Thee, O Lord of lords, O God of gods, O Deva of devas, the Brahman of the Upanishads, the support of Maya, Ishwara, the Supreme Bridge to immortality.

Om Shanti Om Shanti Om Shanti

IV

THE CHRISTIAN REVELATION

The Unity of Mankind

There is but one God the Father, one Logos the Son, and one Spirit and one salvation only for all who believe in him.

... There is but one salvation as there is one God ... There is one only Son who fulfils the will of the Father, and one only human race in which the mysteries of God are fulfilled.

St Irenaeus, Adversus Haereses IV 9.3

This eternal Jesus, the one high priest, intercedes for all men and calls on them: Hearken, he cries, all you peoples, or rather all you who are endowed with reason, barbarians or Greeks! I summon the whole human race, I who am its author by the will of the Father! Come unto me and gather together as one well-ordered unity under the one God and the one Logos of God.

Clement of Alexandria, Protreptikos

Not in vain does John assert that the Word came and dwelt among us, for in this way he teaches us the great mystery that we are all in Christ and that the *common personality of man* is brought back to life by his assuming of it. The new Adam is so called, because he acquires for the common human nature all that pertains to happiness and glory, just as the old Adam acquired all that pertains to its corruption and shame.

St Cyril of Alexandria, *In Joannem Lib.* 1

The whole Christ, if we may be allowed the phrase, the total Christ, is not divided; for he is neither barbarian nor Jew, nor Greek, nor man, nor woman but the new Man wholly transformed by the Spirit.

Clement of Alexandria, *Protrephe* c.11

Paradise

Could any man of sound judgment suppose that the second and third days (of creation) had an evening and a morning when there was as yet no sun or moon or stars? Could anyone be so unintelligent as to think that God made a paradise somewhere in the east and planted it with trees like a farmer, or that in paradise he put a tree of life, a tree you could see and know with your senses, a tree you could derive life from by eating its fruit with the teeth in your head? When the Bible says that God walked in paradise in the evening or that Adam hid behind a tree, no one, I think will question that these are only fictions, stories of things that never actually happened, and that figuratively they refer to certain mysteries.

Origen, *De Principiis*, IV. iii. 1

No one is competent to discuss Adam unless he knows that in Hebrew Adam means 'man'. When Moses talks about Adam, he is talking about human nature. As Scripture testifies, all men have died in Adam and all will be judged as if they had committed Adam's sin. Thus the divine Logos is here speaking not so much about one individual as about the whole human race.

Origen, Contra Celsum, IV. 40

The Incarnation

The mystery of the incarnation of the Word contains in itself the meaning of all the symbols and all the enigmas of Scripture, as well as the hidden meaning of all sensible and intelligible creation. But he who knows the mystery of the Cross and of the tomb knows also the essential principle of all things. Finally he who penetrates yet further and finds himself initiated into the mystery of the resurrection apprehends the end for which God created everything from the beginning.

Maximus the Confessor, Gnostic Centuries 1.66,
quoted in Lessky, Mystical Theology, p. 138

God, Creation, Sin and Redemption

God is not a being, rather he is beyond being and essence. God is pure Monad, that is not that numerical unity which engenders numbers by addition, but rather the source from which the manifold springs forth without altering its absolute simplicity. In as much as it begets multiplicity, the Monad initiates a movement. Owing to this movement of the divinity (Kinesis Theotekos), its being and the nature of its being begin to appear to intellects capable of knowing such objects.

The first movement of the Monad gives rise to the Dyad by generation of the Word who is its total manifestation: then the Monad proceeds up to the Triad by the procession of the Holy Ghost. The first movement of the Monad stops there because its highest manifestation is now perfect ...

This first movement is succeeded by a second by which God manifests himself outside himself in beings that are not God. The Word who is a perfect knowledge of the Monad contains eternally within himself the very being (*ousia*) for all that exists or is ever to exist. Each of these future beings is eternally known, willed and decreed in him to receive existence in due time. God does not make a special decree each time a new being appears. All is eternally contained in the infinite foreknowledge, will and power of God. As objects of the foreknowledge of God these cognitions are called ideas. Each idea is a partial and limited expression of God's perfection; and not only its expression but its manifestation. The production of beings after the pattern of their ideas is called creation. By an effusion of pure goodness the divine Triad radiates those expressions of itself called creatures. The whole of creatures make up a sort of hierarchy where each of them occupies a place determined by its proper degree of perfection...

Originally created on the border line between pure spirits and pure bodies, man was intended to be their connecting link. He was in touch with both the multiplicity of matter by his body and with the unity of God by his mind. His own function, therefore, was to gather up the multiple into the unity of his intellectual knowledge and thus to reunite it with God. In point of fact man did just the contrary; instead of reuniting the multiple by bringing them back to God, he lessened unity by turning away from the knowledge of God to the knowledge of things...

In order to save man from destruction that, whose nature is entirely immobile, or in other words that which moves entirely immovable from within, began to move, so to speak, towards fallen nature in order to create it anew ... God restored human nature to unity by bringing together the natures of body and soul in the person of Christ ...

This union of human and divine nature is the very redemption of man. The end of our restlessness is to rejoin the immutability of God. Now for a mind to move is to know. To move towards God then is to strive to be assimilated to him by knowing him. But God is the good and one cannot know the good without loving it.

In knowing God man begins to love him. Placed out of himself in a kind of ecstasy, he is completely absorbed in his beloved . . . Man is then like unto iron liquefied by fire or like air wholly illumined by the presence of light. Blessed ecstasy when human nature shares in the divine resemblance to the point of becoming that very resemblance, so that without ceasing to be itself, it passes into God. When this happens man no longer lives, rather Christ lives in man.

In thus moving towards God by knowledge and love *man is simply returning to his own idea in God.* Even while he himself is wandering away from God, his idea remains there. Every man is a part of God (*moira theou*) to the extent that by his idea his essence is eternally pre-existent in God. Ecstasy is an earnest of life to come *when the divinization of the universe will be achieved by the return of all things to their eternal ideas*, essences and causes from which they now are separated.

Maximus the Confessor

God

We believe then in one God, one principle (*arche*), having no beginning, uncreated, unbegotten, imperishable and immortal, everlasting, infinite, uncircumscribed, boundless, of infinite power, simple, uncompound, incorporeal, without flux, passionless, unchangeable, unalterable, unseen, the fountain of goodness and justice, the light of the mind, inacces-

sible; a power known by no measure, measurable only
by his own will alone (for all things that he wills, he
can), creator of all created things, seen and unseen,
maintainer and preserver of all, provider for all,
master and lord and king over all, with an endless and
immortal Kingdom: having no contrary, filling all, by
nothing encompassed, but rather himself the encom-
passer and maintainer of all, and original possessor of
the universe, occupying all essences without mixture
(*achrantos*) and extending beyond all things, and
being separate from all essences as being super-essen-
tial, and above all beings and absolute God, absolute
goodness and absolute fullness; determining all sover-
eignties and ranks, being placed above all sovereignty
and rank, above essence and life and word and
thought; being himself very light and goodness and
life and essence, in as much as he does not derive his
being from another, that is to say of those things that
exist: but being himself the fountain of being to all
that is, of life to the living, of reason to those that have
reason, to all the cause of all good: perceiving all
things even before they have begun; one essence, one
divinity, one power, one will, one energy, one beginning, one authority, one dominion, one sovereignty,
made known in three perfect subsistences, and adored
with one worship, believed in and administered to by
all rational creation, united without confusion, and
divided without confusion, and divided without sepa-

ration (which indeed transcends thought).

St John Damascene, *De Fide Orthodoxa*, I. viii

The Unity of Mankind

Brethren, I have already said that Adam was one man and that he was the whole human race. This is what I said if you remember. As though he had been broken and scattered, he is gathered up, and is again made whole in union with others and in spiritual peace.

St Augustine, *In Joannem* X., p.L. XXXV

The whole of human nature is found in Christ by reason of his divinity.

St Thomas, *In III Sent* d. 18 ab. sol 2.

All men descending from Adam may be regarded as one man.

St Thomas, S.T. Ia. Iiae. qu. 81–3,
quoted by Mersch, *Theology of Mystical Body*

Cosmic Revelation

That which is called Christianity existed among the ancients, and never ceased to exist from the beginning of the human race, until Christ came in the flesh, at which time the true religion which already existed began to be called Christianity.

St Augustine

Just as there is no man past, present, or to come, whose nature Jesus Christ has not assumed, so there is no man past, present, or to come, for whom the same Jesus Christ did not undergo his passion.

Council of Carisiacum, 853 AD, *Denziger Euch*. n. 319

I beheld these others beneath Thee and saw that they neither altogether are, nor altogether are not. An existence they have because they are from Thee; and yet no existence because they are not what Thou art. For only that really *is* which remains unchangeably: heaven and earth are beautiful and good and *are* since God made them, but when compared to Thee, they are neither beautiful nor good nor are at all.

St Augustine, *Confessions*, vii. 11

God in Creation

If we say that all things are in God, we understand by this that just as he is without any distinction in his nature, and yet absolutely distinct from all things, thus all things are in him in the greatest distinction and yet not distinct, and first of all because man is God in God: in the same way, then, as God is not distinct from the lion, and yet is altogether distinct from it, so also in God man is not distinct from the lion and yet is absolutely distinct from it. Thus it is also with other things.

(Eckhart, Latin Sermon, IV. 1)

Between the only begotten Son and the soul there is no distinction. This is true. For how could anything white be distinct or divided from whiteness? Again matter and form are one in being, living and working. Yet matter is not on this account form or conversely. So in the proposition, a holy soul is one with God, according to John 17:21. 'That they all may be one in us, even as we are one.' Still the creature is not the creator nor is the just man God.

Now I might ask, how stands it with the soul that is lost in God? Does the soul find herself or not? To this I will answer, as it appears to me, that the soul finds herself in the point where every rational being understands itself. Although it sinks in the eternity of the divine essence, yet it can never reach the ground. Therefore God has left a little point wherein the soul turns back on itself, and knows itself to be a creature.

Eckhart, quoted in *Mysticism - Christian and Buddhist* - by Suzuki

All creatures have existed eternally in the divine essence as in their exemplar. So far as they conform to the divine idea all beings were before their creation one with the essence of God.

Suso

Man was everlasting in God, before he was created, and when he was in God, man was God in God.

John Tauler, Sermon XLIV - Second Sermon on Nativity of St John the Baptist

If the soul knows God in his creatures, that is only evening light; if it knows his creatures in God, that is morning light; if it knows God as He who alone is Being, that is the clear light of midday.

Eckhart, quoted by Otto, *Mysticism East and West*, p. 22

Brethren, even before this sensible world was made, there was then no less being than there is now. It existed but in a much simpler state than we now find it. Everything we see in creation must necessarily have come from its exemplar. But it is not yet true that all that was in the exemplar must have come into creation. In the exemplar not only all that has been created, but all that can ever be created, *exist more beautifully and more truly. There things are truth and life*. We know things in their sensible (perceptible) state, but *their supreme existence is in that archetype*, of which it is written, that it reacheth from one end to the other mightily and ordereth all things sweetly.

Isaac of Stalla, Sermon XXIV, quoted in Bonyer,
The Cistercian Heritage

Religion where it is in truth and in power renews the very spirit of our minds and doth in a manner spiritualize this outward creation to us. It teaches the soul to look at those perfections it finds here below, not so much as perfections of this or that body, as they adorn this or that particular being, but as they are so many rays issuing forth from that first and essential

Perfection in which they all meet and embrace one another in the most close friendship. Every particular good is a blossom of the first Goodness: every created excellency is a beam descending from the Father of Lights: and should we separate all these particularities from God, all affection spent on them would be unchaste. We should love all things in God and God in all things, because He is All in all, the beginning and origin of their being, the perfect idea of their Goodness and the end of their motion . . .

There is a twofold meaning in every creature, a literal and a mystical, and the one is but the ground of the other.

God made the universe and all the creatures contained therein as so many glasses wherein he might reflect His own glory. He hath copied Himself forth in creation . . . How to find God here and feelingly converse with Him, and being affected with the sense of the Divine Glory shining out upon the creation, how to pass out of the sensible world into the intellectual is effectually taught by true religion.

God hath stamped a copy of His own archetypal loveliness on the soul, that man by reflecting into himself might behold there the glory of God . . . Reason in man being *lumen de lumine*, a light flowing from the fountain and Father of lights . . .

Moses-like conversing with God on the mount and there beholding His glory shining out upon us in the face of Christ, we should be deriving a copy of that eternal beauty upon our souls, and our thirsty and hungry spirits would be perpetually sucking in a true participation and image of His glory.

When reason once is raised by the mighty force of the Divine Spirit into a converse with God, it is turned into sense . . . We shall then converse with God *toinnoi*, whereas before we conversed with Him only *teidianoiai* with our discursive faculty.

John Smith, *The Excellency and Nobleness of True Religion etc.* quoted by E. I. Watkin in *Poets and Mystics*

There is a spirit that delights to do no evil, not to revenge any wrong, but delights to endure all things in hope to enjoy its own in the end. Its hope is to outlive all wrath and contention, and to weary out all exaltation and cruelty, or whatever is of a nature contrary to itself. It sees to the end of all temptations. As it bears no evil in itself, so it conceives none in thought to any other. If it be betrayed, it bears it, for its ground and spring is the mercies and forgiveness of God. Its crown is meekness, its life is everlasting love unfeigned; it takes its kingdom with entreaty and not with contention, and keeps it by lowliness of mind.

James Nayler, written two hours before his death

The divine light is Christ within the human soul, and is as universal as the seed of sin. All men, heathen as well as Christian, are endowed with the divine light, even though they may know nothing of the outward history of Christ's life. Justification is for those who do not resist the Inner Light and so permit of a new birth of holiness in them.

Robert Barclay, quoted in *The Perennial Philosophy*

If we would speak correctly we must confess on the authority of the Bible itself, that all knowledge of religion is from Him, and not only that which the Bible has transmitted to us. There never was a time when God had not spoken to man and told him to a certain extent his duty. His injunctions to Noah, the common father of all mankind, is the first recorded fact of the sacred history after the Deluge. Accordingly we are expressly told in the New Testament that at no time he left himself without witness in the world, and that in every nation he accepts those who fear and obey Him. It would seem, then, that there is something true and divinely revealed in all religion all over the earth, overloaded, as it may be, at times even stifled by the impieties which the corrupt will and understanding of man have incorporated with it. Such are the doctrines of the power and presence of an invisible God, of his moral law and governance, of the obligation of duty and certainly of moral judgment, and of reward and punishment as eventually dispensed to individuals; so that Revelation properly speaking, is a universal not local gift; and the distinction between the state of Israelites formerly, and Christians now, and that of the heathen, is not that we can and they cannot attain to future blessedness, but that the Church of God ever has had, and the rest of mankind never have had, authoritative documents of truth and appointed channels of communication with him. The Word and the Sacrament are the characteristics of the elect people of God, but all men have had more or less the guidance of tradition, in addition to those internal notions of right and wrong which the Spirit has put into each. This vague and uncertain family of religious truths, originally from God but sojourning in the world without the sanction of miracle, or a definite home, as pilgrims up and down the world, and discernible and separate from the corrupt legends with which they are mixed by the spiritual mind alone, may be called the Dispensation of Paganism . . .

Newman, *Arians of the Fourth Century*

The Human Person

The person is of all beings the most firmly and perfectly existent. Stones, plants, even animals, really exist, but their existence is provisional, precarious and finally not very emphatically differentiated: whereas the human person exists in himself and by himself and for himself. This supreme mode of existence we shall here call subsistence. A thing that exists *in* itself is one that exists without having to adhere in another subject, with no merely borrowed being, but one that suffices to itself because centred on itself. A thing that exists *by* itself is one that exists as being its own source, as positing itself in being by its own internal and unfailing power, and as possessing its own being in a substantial and exclusive manner. A thing that exists *for* itself is one that has meaning and a value of its own, which is ordered to itself, which is an end, with an absolute, definitive and unique character in the universe. The spirit, and the spirit alone, is the principle of this full subsistence, because it is simple, wholly identical with itself, and constituting a totality and a universe in its own sole self. So true is this, that thus to subsist by itself, in virtue of itself, is to 'return to its own essence', or in other words to coincide with itself, to be present to itself, and therefore to be capable of knowing itself by way of reflection. Subsistence by itself, return on self, consciousness of self – three terms of necessity linked with each other, because they define the structure of the spirit . . .

But all is not yet said. An analysis that went no further would stop too soon. It is correct enough on its own plane, but incomplete: for the person exists for an end, and is not to be fully accounted for, if this datum is neglected. Moreover, it falls short in itself, for if the person really exists in, by, and for himself, this has to be taken in an altogether relative sense. He subsists, but he is open; and open in a two-fold direction.

In the first place his subsistence is borrowed; it is

continuously communicated, wholly participated. It may be said then to be a relation to the First Subsistence, in which it participates, to the Pure Act who communicates Himself, to the Being who gives and loses nothing because He is pure Existence. If then the person is resistant, absolute, closed on himself, he is all this in virtue of another; and in all, that makes him what he is – subsistent, distinct, incommunicable – he bears a relation to God. An internal relation, because it links up the person with God as with the immanent principle of his total being; a constitutive relation, because it expresses nothing alien but his very being as participated; and an immediate relation, because no intermediary is here possible, or even conceivable, and because nothing can be at all without drawing directly on the unique source of all beings. *Thus the person is necessarily a subsistent relation to God.* In the case of man we can even put a finger on the precise point at which the relation is inserted. Not in the composite of soul and body as such, since it is not through matter or anything that follows from matter, that God touches the human being; but only through the spiritual principle, through the soul itself, by giving the soul this *esse*, which is the act of every subsistent form and so also the unique act of the man in his entirety. It is in virtue of this actuality, immediately, totally and enduringly participated, that the person appears as a spiritual and subsistent relation to God . . .

If man exists in himself, by himself and for himself, it is because he participates in a certain plenitude and concentration of being which are proper to God: and because he imitates, poorly enough no doubt, the simple perfection of God. Far from being something that isolates the person, and shuts him up in himself, this possession of self by self, this return of self on self, is on the contrary something that links him up closer with and brings him more under the sway of Subsistent Being itself, since it is a divine mark ceaselessly participated by God. *The more the person exists in himself incommunicable and perfect, so much the more he receives from, so much the more he depends on God . . .*

The person subsists in a spiritual nature. Now this nature is at once individual and specific: individual as belonging to a given person: specific because open to the whole species. The person subsists in *a* nature which is in relationship with *the* nature. The nature here in question is not to be envisaged either as a subsistent idea – such a realism of essences becomes superfluous as soon as the Creator is admitted – nor yet as a pure object of thought – for so we would retain the concept only and not the *res* of human nature – nor yet again as a reality purely individualized in a human person, since in this sense it is closed and incommunicable; but as a reality present in all individuals of the human species. In this sense the nature surpasses, englobes and unifies all the individuals; and this is the standpoint we shall have to adopt, if we want to understand the real history of humanity, and, to begin with, the real meaning of the human person. Through this nature *in* which he subsists the person is in contact with the entire human species; *he is immanent in the species, and the species is immanent in him.*

In a sense what is here first is the species, the human race envisaged as an organic whole. *The whole corresponds to the creative idea which posited humanity and being,* and which multiplies man in space and time to bring humanity to realization . . . For humanity develops through persons, and does so only by communicating itself to this person or to that, and through this person to that. *In virtue of their unity in the species, all men form but a single man – omnes homines, unus homo.* And human nature appears as a force which propagates itself from man to man, from the first man to the last, until the human idea shall be fully achieved, until humanity shall be consummated, until the divine likeness, which is the final goal of every species and the immediate end of humanity, shall be fully unfolded for ever . . .

But this, inevitable and evident as it is, conceals a yet deeper truth. The man is not simply immanent in the species as a part within a whole and a member in a body. The Whole in its turn is found in the part, the species in the member, the nature in each nature, humanity in each man. There we have an even more radical immanence, which brings us this time into the very heart of the person, and compels us to balance our formula: *omnes homines, unus homo,* by this other one: *unus homo, omnes homines.*

Mouroux, The Meaning of Man

V

THE WAY OF MYSTICISM

Poems of Kabir

I

The light of the sun and the moon and the stars shines
   bright:
The melody of love swells forth, and the rhythm of
   love's detachment beats the time.
Day and night the chorus of music fills the heavens; and
   Kabir says: 'My beloved One gleams like the lightning flash in the sky.'

Do you know how the moments perform their adora-
   tion?
Waving its row of lamps, the universe sings in worship
   day and night.
There are the hidden banner and the secret canopy.
There the sound of the unseen bells is heard.
Kabir says: 'There adoration never ceases; there the
   Lord of the Universe sitteth on his throne.

The whole world does its works and commits its errors:
   but few are the lovers who know the Beloved.
The devout seeker is he who mingles in his heart the

double currents of love and detachment, like the mingling of the streams of Ganges and Jumna;
In his heart the sacred water flows day and night; and thus the round of births and deaths is brought to an end.

Behold what wonderful rest is in the Supreme Spirit! and he enjoys it, who makes himself meek for it.
Held by the cords of love, the swing of the Ocean of Joy sways to and fro; and a mighty sound breaks forth in song.
See what a lotus blooms there without water! and Kabir says: 'My heart's bee drinks its nectar.'

What a wonderful lotus it is that, blooms at the heart of the spinning wheel of the universe! Only a few pure souls know of its true delight.
Music is all around it, and there the heart partakes of the joy of the infinite sea.
Kabir says: 'Dive thou into that Ocean of sweetness: thus let all errors of life and of death flee away.'

Behold how the thirst of the five senses is quenched there! and the three forms of misery are no more!
Kabir says: 'It is the sport of the Unattainable One: look within and see how the moonbeams of that Hidden One shine in you.'

There falls the rhythmic beat of life and death:
Rapture wells forth, and all space is radiant with light.
There the Unstruck Music is sounded; it is the music of

the love of the three worlds.
There millions of lamps of sun and of moon are
    burning;
There the drum beats, and the lover smugs in play.
There the love-song resounds, and light rain in showers;
    and the worshipper is entranced in the taste of heav-
    enly nectar.
Look upon life and death; there is no separation
    between them;
The right hand and the left hand are one and the same.
Kabir says: 'There the wise man is speechless: for this
    truth may never be found in Vedas or in books.'

I have had my seat on the Self-poised One,
I have drunk of the cup of the Ineffable,
I have found the Key of the Mystery,
I have reached the Root of Union.
Travelling by no track I have come to the Sorrowless
    Land: very easily has the mercy of the great Lord
    come upon me.
They have sung of Him as infinite and unattainable: but
    I in my meditations have seen him without sight.
That is indeed the sorrowless land, and none knows the
    path that leads there:
Only he who is on that path has surely transcended all
    sorrow.
Wonderful is that land of rest, to which no merit can
    win;

It is the wise who has seen it, it is the wise who has sung of it.

This is the Ultimate Word: but can any express its marvellous savour?

He who has savoured it once, he knows what joy it can give.

Kabir says: 'Knowing it the ignorant man becomes wise, and the wise man becomes speechless and silent,

The worshipper is utterly inebriated,

His wisdom and detachment are made perfect;

He drinks from the cup of the inbreathings and the outbreathings of love.'

There the whole sky is filled with sound, and there that music is made without fingers and without strings;

There the game of pleasure and pain does not cease.

Kabir says: 'If you merge your life in the Ocean of Life, you will find your life in the Supreme Land of Bliss.'

What a frenzy of ecstasy there is in every hour! and the worshipper is pressing out and drinking the essence of the hours, he lives the life of Brahma.

I speak truth for I have accepted truth in life; I am now attached to truth, I have swept all tinsel away.

Kabir says: 'Thus is the worshipper set free from fear. thus have all errors of life and of death left him.'

There the sky is filled with music:

There it rains nectar:

There the harp-strings jingle, and there the drums beat.

What a secret splendour is there in the mansion of the sky!

There no mention is made of the rising and the setting of the sun;

In the ocean of manifestation which is the light of love, day and night are felt to be one.

Joy for ever, no sorrow, no struggle!

There have I seen joy filled to the brim, perfection of joy;

No place for error is there.

Kabir says: 'There have I witnessed the sport of One Bliss.'

I have known in my body the sport of the universe: I have escaped from the error of this world.

The inward and the outward are become as one sky, the Infinite and the finite united: I am drunken with the sight of this ALL!

This Light of Thine fills the universe: the lamp of love that burns on the salver of knowledge.

Kabir says: 'There error cannot enter, and the conflict of life and death is felt no more.'

II

The shadows of evening fall thick and deep and the darkness of love envelops the body and the mind.

Open the window to the west and be lost in the sky of love;

Drink the sweet honey that steeps the petals of the lotus
of the heart.

Receive the waves in your body: what splendour is in
the region of the sea!

Hark! The sound of conches and bells are rising.

Kabir says: 'O brother, behold! the Lord is in the vessel
of my body.'

III

More than all else do I cherish at heart that love which
makes me to live a limitless life in this world.

It is like the lotus which lives in the water and blooms in
the water: yet the water cannot touch its petals, they
open beyond its reach.

It is like a wife who enters the fire at the bidding of love.
She burns and lets others grieve, but never dishon-
ours love.

This ocean of the world is hard to cross: its waters are
very deep.

Kabir says: 'Listen to me, O Sadhu! few there are who
have reached its end.'

IV

My Lord hides himself and my Lord wonderfully
reveals himself:

My Lord has encompassed me with hardness and my
Lord has cast down my limitations.

My Lord brings to me words of sorrow and words of
joy, and He Himself heals their strife.

I will offer my body and my mind to my Lord: I will give
up my life, but never can I forget my Lord!

V

A sore pain troubles me day and night, and I cannot
sleep;
I long for the meeting with my beloved and my father's
house gives me pleasure no more.
The gates of the sky are opened, the temple is revealed:
I meet my husband, and leave at his feet the offering of
my body and my mind.

VI

He who is meek and contented, he who has an equal
vision, whose mind is filled with the fullness of acceptance and of rest;
He who has seen Him and touched Him, he is freed
from all fear and trouble. To him the perpetual
thought of God is like sandal paste smeared on the
body, to him nothing else is delight.
His work and his rest are filled with music: he sheds
abroad the radiance of love.
Kabir says: 'Touch his feet, who is one and indivisible,
immutable and peaceful: who fills all vessels to the
brim with joy and whose form is love.'

VII

O Sadhu, the simple union is the best.
Since the day when I met with my Lord, there has been

no end to the sport of our love.

I shut not my eyes, I close not my ears, I do not mortify my body;

I see with open eyes and smile and behold His beauty everywhere:

I utter His name and whatever I see, it reminds me of Him; whatever I do, it becomes His worship.

The rising and the setting are one to me: all contradictions are solved.

Whenever I go, I move round Him,

All I achieve is His service:

When I lie down, I lie prostrate at His feet.

He is the only adorable one to me: I have none other.

My tongue has left off impure words, it sings his glory night and day:

Whether I rise or sit down, I can never forget him: for the rhythm of his music beats in my ears.

Kabir says: 'My heart is frenzied and I disclose in my soul what is hidden.

I am immersed in that one great bliss, which transcends all pleasure and pain.'

VIII

The flute of the Infinite is played without ceasing and its sound is love.

When love renounces all limits it reaches truth.

How widely the fragrance spreads! It has no end, nothing stands in its way. The form of this melody is bright like a million suns: incomparably sounds the vina, the vina of the notes of truth.

IX

Subtle is the path of love.

Therein is no asking and no not-asking.

There one loses oneself at His feet.

There one is immersed in the joy of the seeking: plunged in the deeps of love as the fish in the water.

The lover is never slow in offering his head for his Lord's service.

Kabir declares the secret of this love.

X

He is the real Sadhu who can reveal the form of the Formless to the vision of these eyes:

Who teaches the simple way of attaining Him, which is other than rites or ceremonies.

Who does not make you close the doors or hold the breath, and renounce the world.

Who makes you perceive the Supreme Spirit whenever the mind attaches itself: Who teaches you to be still in the midst of all your activities.

Ever immersed in bliss, having no fear in his mind, he keeps the spirit of union in the midst of all enjoyments.

The infinite dwelling of the Infinite Being is everywhere: in earth, water, sky, air:

Firm as the thunderbolt, the seal of the seeker is

established above the void.

He who is within is without: I see Him and none else.

XI

Receive that Word from which the Universe springeth!
    That word is the Master; I have heard it and become
    the disciple.

How many are there who know the meaning of that
    Word?

The Vedas and the Puranas proclaim it.

The world is established in it.

The Rishis and the devotees speak of it:

But none knows the mystery of the Word.

The householder leaves his house when he hears it,

The ascetic comes back to love when he hears it,

The Six Philosophies expound it,

The Spirit of Renunciation points to that Word,

From that Word the world – form has sprung,

That Word reveals all.

Kabir says: 'But who knows whence the Word cometh?'

XII

Why so impatient, my heart?

He who watches over birds and beasts and insects,

He who cared for you whilst you were yet in your
    mother's womb,

Shall He not care for you now that you are come forth?

Oh my heart, how could you turn from the smile of
    your Lord and wander so far from Him?

You have left your Beloved and are thinking of others;
and this is why all your work is in vain.

XIII

O my heart! You have not known all the secrets of this
city of love: in ignorance you came and in ignorance
you return.

O my friend! What have you done with this life? You
have taken on your head the heavy burden of stones,
and who is to lighten it for you?

Your Friend stands on the other shore, but you never
think in your mind how you may meet Him:

The boat is broken and yet you sit ever upon the bank;
and thus you are beaten to no purpose by the waves.

The servant Kabir asks you to consider; who is there
that shall be your friend at the last?

You are alone, you have no companion. You will suffer
the consequences of your own deeds.

XIV

Open your eyes of love and see Him who pervades this
world!

Consider it well and know that this is your own
country.

When you meet the true Master, He will awaken your
heart;

He will tell you the secret of love and detachment, and
then you will know indeed that He transcends the
universe.

This world is the City of Truth, its maze of paths
  enchants the heart:
We can reach the goal without crossing the road, such is
  the sport unending.
Where the ring of manifold joys ever dances about Him,
  there is the sport of Eternal Bliss.
When we know this, then all our receiving and
  renouncing is over;
Thenceforth the heat of having shall never scorch us
  more.

He is the Ultimate Rest unbounded:
He has spread His form of love throughout the world.
From that Ray which is Truth, streams of new forms are
  perpetually springing: and He pervades those forms.
All the gardens and groves and bowers are abounding
  with blossom; and the air breaks forth into ripples of
  joy.
There the swan plays a wonderful game.
There the unstruck music eddies around the Infinite
  One.
There in the midst the throne of the Unheld is shining
  whereon the great Being sits.
Millions of suns are shamed by the radiance of a single
  hair of His body.
On the harp of the road what true melodies are being
  sounded! and its notes pierce the heart:
There the eternal Fountain is playing its endless life-

streams of birth and death.

They call Him Emptiness who is the Truth of truths, on Whom all truths are stored!

There within Him creation goes forward, which is beyond all philosophy: for philosophy cannot attain to Him:

There is an endless world, O my brother! and there is the Nameless Being of whom nought can be said.

No form, no body, no length, no breadth is seen there: how can I tell you that which it is?

He comes to the path of the Infinite on whom the grace of the Lord descends: he is freed from births and deaths, who attains to Him.

Kabir says: 'It cannot be told by the words of the mouth, it cannot be written on paper:

It is like a dumb person who tastes a sweet thing – how shall it be explained?'

XV

To whom shall I go to learn about my Beloved?

Kabir says: 'As you never may find the forest if you ignore the tree, so He may never be found in abstractions.'

How we achieve supernatural sight in our inward workings

Christ says: Behold. Whosoever wishes to see in a supernatural way in his inward exercises must have three things. The first is the light of Divine grace, and this is in a more lofty degree than that which we can experience in the outward and active life without earnest inward diligence. The second thing is the casting out of all distracting images and attachments from the heart; so that the man may be free and image-less, released from all attachments, and empty of all creatures. The third thing is a free turning of the will, with a gathering together of all our powers, both bodily and spiritual, cleansed from every inordinate love. Thereby the will flows forth into the unity of God and into the unity of the mind; and thus the rational creature may obtain and possess the most high unity of God in a supernatural manner. For this God has created heaven and earth and everything; and for this reason he became man, and taught us; and lived for our sake, and has Himself become the Way to the unity. And He died in the bonds of love, and ascended and has opened to us that very unity; in which we may possess eternal bliss.

John of Ruysbroeck, *Adornment of the Spiritual Marriage*

Of a threefold Unity which is in us by Nature

The first and highest unity of man is in God; for all creatures depend upon this unity far their being, their life,
and their preservation; and if they be separated in this
wise from God, they fall into the nothingness and
became nought. This unity is in us essentially, by
nature, whether we be good or evil. And without our
own working it makes us neither holy nor blessed. This
unity we possess within us and yet above us, as the
ground and the preserver of our being and of our life.

The second unity or union is also in us by nature. It is
the unity of our higher powers; for as much as these
spring naturally as active powers from the unity of the
mind or of the spirit. This is that same unity which
depends upon God; but with this difference, that here it
is active and there essential. Nevertheless, the spirit is
wholly and perfectly understood according to the fullness, of its substance, in each unity. This unity we
possess within us, above our senses; and from it there
proceed memory, understanding, and will, and all the
powers of spiritual action. In this unity, the soul is
called 'spirit'.

The third unity which is in us by nature is the source
of all the bodily powers, in the unity of the heart; origin
and beginning of the bodily life. This unity the soul
possesses in the body and in the quickening centre of
the heart, and therefrom flow forth all bodily activities,

111

and the five senses. And therein the soul is called 'soul'; for it is the forming principle of the body, and quickens this carcass; that is, gives it life and keeps it therein.

These three unities abide in man by nature as one life and one kingdom. In the lowest we are sensible and animal; in the middle we are rational and spiritual; and in the highest we are kept according to our essence. And thus are all men by nature.

Of the Unity of the Divine Nature in the Trinity of the Persons

The most high and superessential Unity of the Divine Nature, where the Father and the Son possess Their nature in the unity of the Holy Spirit – above the comprehension and understanding of all our powers, in the naked being of our spirit – is a supernal stillness, wherein God broods above all creatures in the created light. This most high Unity of the Divine Nature is living and fruitful; for out of this same Unity, the Eternal Word is incessantly born of the Father. And, through this birth, the Father knows the Son; and in the Son, all things. And the Son knows the Father; and all things in the Father. For they are one Simple Nature. From this mutual contemplation of the Father and the Son, in the eternal radiance, there flow forth an eternal contentment and a fathomless love, and that is the Holy Spirit. And through the Holy Spirit, and through the Eternal Wisdom, God inclines Himself towards each creature in particular, and lovingly endows and enkindles each one, according to its worth and the state into which it has been put and to which it has been destined by its virtues and by the Eternal Providence of God. And thereby all good spirits, in heaven and on earth, are moved to virtue and righteousness.

Of the third coming of Christ

Through this loving inclination of God, and His inward working in the unity of our spirit, and further through our glowing love and the pressing of all our powers together into the very unity in which God dwells, there arises the third coming of Christ in inward working. And this is an inward touch or stirring of Christ in His Divine brightness, in the inmost part of our spirit. The second coming, of which we have spoken, we have likened to a fountain, pouring forth in three rills. But this coming will liken to the duct which feeds the fountain. For there is no rill without a fountain; and no fountain without a living duct. So likewise the grace of God flows forth like rills into the higher powers, and impels and enkindles a man in all virtue. And this grace springs up within the unity of our spirit like a fountain, and falls back again into that same unity whence it arises; even as a living and gushing spring which comes forth from the living ground of the Divine Richness, where neither faithfulness nor grace can ever fail. And this is the touch which I mean. And the creature passively endures this touch. For here there is a union of the higher powers within the unity of the spirit, above the multiplicity of all the virtues, and here no one works save God alone, in untrammelled goodness; which is the cause of all our virtues and of all blessedness. In the unity of the spirit, into which this duct gushes forth, one is above activity and above reason, though not without reason. For the enlightened reason, and especially the power of love, feels this touch; and reason cannot understand, nor can it comprehend, the way or the means of this touch, how or what it is, for it is a working of God, the upspringing and the inrushing of all graces and gifts, and the last intermediary between God and the creature. And above this touch, in the still being of the spirit, there broods an incomprehensible Brightness. And that is the most high Trinity whence this touch proceeds. There God lives and reigns in the spirit, and the spirit in God.

Of the essential Meeting with God without Means in the Nakedness of our Nature

Now understand and mark this well. The unity of our spirit has two conditions: it is essential, and it is active. You must know that the spirit, according to its essence, receives the coming of Christ in the nakedness of its nature, without means and without interruption. For the being and the life which we are in God, in our Eternal Image, and which we have within ourselves according to our essence, this is without means and indivisible. And this is why the spirit, in its inmost and highest part, that is in its naked nature, receives without interruption the impress of its Eternal Archetype, and the Divine Brightness; and is an eternal dwelling-place of God in which God dwells as an eternal Presence, and which He visits perpetually, with new comings and with new instreamings of the ever-renewed brightness of His eternal birth. For where He comes, there He is; and where He is, there He comes. And where He has never been, thereto He shall never come; for neither chance nor change are in Him. And everything in which He is, is in Him; for He never goes out of Himself. And this is why the spirit in its essence possesses God in the nakedness of its nature, as God does the spirit: for it lives in God and God in it. And it is able, in its highest part, to receive, without intermediary, the Brightness of God, and all that God can fulfill. And by means of the brightness of its Eternal Archetype, which shines in it essentially and personally, the spirit plunges itself and loses itself, as regards the highest part of its life, in the Divine Being, and there abidingly possesses its eternal blessedness; and it flows forth again, through the eternal birth of the Son, together with all the other creatures, and is set in its created being by the free will of the Holy Trinity. And here it is like unto the image of the most high Trinity in Unity, in which it has been made. And, in its created being, it incessantly receives the impress of its

Eternal Archetype, like a flawless mirror, in which the image remains steadfast, and in which the reflection is renewed without interruption by its ever-new reception in new light. This essential union of our spirit with God does not exist in itself, but it dwells in God, and it flows forth from God, and it depends upon God, and it returns to God as to its Eternal Origin. And in this wise it has never, nor ever shall be, separated from God; for this union is within us by our naked nature, and were this nature to be separated from God, it would fall into pure nothingness. And this union is above time and space, and is always incessantly active according to the way of God. But our nature, forasmuch as it is indeed like unto God but in itself is creature, receives the impress of its Eternal Image passively. This is that nobleness which we possess by nature in the essential unity of our spirit, where it is united with God according to nature. This neither makes us holy nor blessed, for all men, whether good or evil, possess it within themselves; but it is certainly the first cause of all holiness and all blessedness. This is the meeting and the union between God and our spirit in the nakedness of our nature.

How our Spirit is called to go out in Contemplation and Fruition

Now the Spirit of God says in the secret outpouring of our spirit: Go ye, go, in an eternal contemplation and fruition, according to the way of God. All the riches which are in God by nature we possess by way of love in God, and God in us, through the unmeasured love which is the Holy Spirit; for in this love one tastes of all that one can desire. And therefore through this love we are dead to ourselves, and have gone forth in loving immersion into Waylessness and Darkness. There the spirit is embraced by the Holy Trinity, and dwells for ever within the superessential Unity, in rest and fruition. And in that same Unity, according to Its fruitfulness, the Father dwells in the Son, and the Son in the Father, and all creatures dwell in Both. And this is above the distinction of the Persons; for here by means of the reason we understand Fatherhood and Sonhood as the life-giving fruitfulness of the Divine Nature.

Here there arise and begin an eternal going out and an eternal work which is without beginning; for here there is a beginning with beginning. For, after the Almighty Father had perfectly comprehended Himself in the ground of His fruitfulness, so the Son, the Eternal Word of the Father, came forth as the second Person in the Godhead. And through the Eternal Birth, all creatures have come forth in eternity, before they were created in time. So God has seen and known them in Himself, according to distinction, in living ideas, and in an otherness from Himself, but not as something other in all ways, for all that is in God is God. This eternal going out and this eternal life, which we have and are in God eternally, without ourselves, is the cause of our

117

created being in time. And our created being abides in the Eternal Essence, and is one with it in its essential existence. And this eternal life and being, which we have and are in the eternal Wisdom of God, is like unto God. For it has an eternal immanence in the Divine Essence, without distinction; and through the birth of the Son it has an eternal outflowing in a distinction and otherness, according to the Eternal Idea. And through these two points it is so like unto God that He knows and reflects Himself in this likeness without cessation, according to the Essence and according to the Persons. For, though even here there are distinction and otherness according to intellectual perception, yet this likeness is one with that same Image of the Holy Trinity, which is the wisdom of God and in which God beholds Himself and all things in an eternal Now, without before and after. In a single seeing He beholds himself and all things. And this is the Image and the Likeness of God, and our Image and our Likeness; for in it God reflects Himself and all things. In this Divine Image all creatures have an eternal life, outside themselves, as in their eternal Archetype; and after this eternal Image, and in this Likeness, we have been made by the Holy Trinity. And therefore God wills that we shall go forth from ourselves in this Divine Light, and shall reunite ourselves in a supernatural way with this Image, which is our proper life, and shall possess it with Him, in action and in fruition in eternal bliss.

For we know well that the bosom of the Father is our ground and origin, in which we begin our being and our life. And from our proper ground, that is from the Father and from all that lives in Him, there shines forth an eternal brightness, which is the birth of the Son. And in this brightness that is, in the Son, the Father knows Himself and all that lives in Him; for all that He has, and all that He is, He gives to the Son, save only the property of Fatherhood, which abides in Himself. And this is why all that lives in the Father, unmanifested in the Unity, is also in the Son actively poured forth into manifestation: and the simple ground of our Eternal Image ever remains in darkness and in waylessness, but the brightness without limit which streams forth from it, this reveals and brings forth within the Conditioned the hiddenness of God. And all those men who are raised up above their created being into a God-seeing life are one with this Divine brightness. And they are that brightness itself, and they see, feel, and find, even by means of this Divine Light, that, as regards their uncreated essence, they are that same onefold ground from which the brightness without limit shines forth in the Divine way, and which, according to the simplicity of the Essence, abides eternally onefold and wayless within. And this is why inward and God-seeing men will go out in the way of contemplation, above reason and above distinction and above their created being, through an eternal intuitive gazing. By means of this

inborn light they are transfigured, and made one with
that same light through which they see and which they
see. And thus the God-seeing men follow after their
Eternal Image, after which they have been made; and
they behold God and all things, without distinction, in
a simple seeing, in the Divine brightness. And this is the
most noble and the most profitable contemplation to
which one can attain in this life; for in this contemplation, a man best remains master of himself and free.
And at each loving introversion he may grow in nobility
of life beyond anything that we are able to understand;
for he remains free and master of himself in inwardness
and virtue. And this gazing at the Divine Light holds
him up above all inwardness and all virtue and all
merit, for it is the crown and the reward after which we
strive, and which we have and possess now in this wise;
for a God-seeing life is a heavenly life. But were we set
free from this misery and this exile, so we should have,
as regards our created being, a greater capacity to
receive this brightness; and so the glory of God would
shine through us in every way better and more nobly.
This is the way above all ways, in which one goes out
through Divine contemplation and an eternal intuitive
gazing, and in which one is transfigured and trans-
muted in the Divine brightness. This going out of the
God-seeing man is also in love; for through the fruition
of love he rises above his created being, and finds and
tastes the riches and the delights which are God

Himself, and which He causes to pour forth without interruption in the hiddenness of the spirit, where the spirit is like unto the nobility of God.

Of a Divine Meeting which takes place in the Hiddenness of our Spirit

When the inward and God-seeing man has thus attained to his Eternal Image, and in this clearness, through the Son, has entered into the bosom of the Father; then he is enlightened by Divine truth, and he, receives anew, every moment, the Eternal Birth, and he goes forth according to the way of the light in a Divine contemplation. And here there begins the fourth and last point; namely, a loving meeting, in which, above all else, our highest blessedness consists.

You should know that the Heavenly Father, as a living ground, with all that lives in Him, is actively turned towards His Son, as to His own Eternal Wisdom. And that same Wisdom, with all that lives in It, is actively turned back towards the Father, that is, towards that very ground from which It comes forth. And in this meeting, there comes forth the third Person, between the Father and the Son; that is the Holy Spirit, Their mutual Love, who is one with them both in the same nature. And he enfolds and drenches through both in action and fruition the Father and the Son, and all that lives in Both, with such great riches and such joy that as to this all creatures must eternally be silent; for the incomprehensible wonder of this love, eternally transcends the understanding of all creatures. But where this wonder is understood and tasted without amazement, there the spirit dwells above itself, and is one with the Spirit of God; and tastes and sees without measure, even as God, the riches which are the spirit itself in the unity of the living ground, where it possesses itself according to the way of its uncreated essence.

Now this rapturous meeting is incessantly and actively renewed in us, according to the way of God; for the Father gives Himself in the Son, and the Son gives Himself in the Father, in an eternal content and a loving embrace; and this renews itself every moment within the bonds of love. For like as the Father incessantly beholds all things in the birth of His Son, so all things are loved anew by the Father and the Son in the outpouring of the Holy Spirit. And this is the active meeting of the Father and of the Son, in which we are lovingly embraced by the Holy Spirit in eternal love.

Now this active meeting and this loving embrace are in their ground fruitive and wayless; for the abysmal Waylessness of God is so dark and unconditioned that it swallows up in itself every Divine way and activity, and all the attributes of the Persons, within the rich compass of the essential Unity; and it brings about a Divine fruition in the abyss of the Ineffable. And here there is a death in fruition, and a melting and dying into the

Essential Nudity, where all the Divine names, and all conditions, and all the living images which are reflected in the mirror of Divine Truth, lapse in the Onefold and Ineffable, in waylessness and without reason. For in this unfathomable abyss of the Simplicity, all things are wrapped in fruitive bliss; and the abyss itself may not be comprehended, unless by Essential Unity. To this the Persons, and all that lives in God, must give place; for here there is nought else but an eternal rest in the fruitive embrace of an outpouring Love. And this is that wayless being which all interior spirits have chosen above all other things. This is the dark silence in which all lovers lose themselves. But if we would prepare ourselves for it by means of the virtues, we should strip ourselves of all but our very bodies, and should flee forth into the wild Sea, whence no created thing can draw us back again.

BEDE GRIFFITHS INTERNATIONAL
CONTEMPLATION CENTRES

Osage Monastery
Sr M Pascaline Coff O.S.B.
18701 W. Monastery Rd.
USA – Sand Springs, OK 74063
Ph: 001–918–245–2734
Fax: 001–918–245–9360

New Camaldoli Hermitage
Fr Robert Hale O.S.B. Cam.
USA – Big Sur, CA 93920
Ph: 001–408–667–0480
Fax: 001–408–667–0480
        (Fr Robert Hale pers.)
        001–408–667–0209
        (Fr Robert Bruno)

Monastero di S. Gregorio Magno
Fr Bernadino Cozzarini O.S.B.
    Cam.
Piazza di S. Gregorio al Celio #1
1–00184 Roma, Italia
Ph: 01139–6–700–8227
Fax: 01139–6–700–9357

Epiphany Monastery
Fr Romuald O.S.B. Cam.
P.O. Box 60
USA – New Boston, NH 03070
Ph: 001–603–487–3020
Fax: 001–603–487–3700

Saccidananda Ashram –
    Shantivanam
Br John Martin Kuvarapu
O.S.B. Cam.
Tannirpalli 639–107
Kulittalai, Tiruchy District
Tamil Nadu, South INDIA
Ph: 01191–4323–3060
Fax: 01191–4323–4014

Christ by the River Hermitage
Fr Douglas Conlan Obl. O.S.B.
P.O. Box 35
Pinjarra 6208 – W. Australia
Ph: 01161–9–531–1227
Fax: 01161–9–531–2480

Shantigiri/Mount of Peace/
  Berg des Friedens
Roland R. Ropers Obl. O.S.B.
Gräfin-Schlippenbach–Weg 16
D – 83708 Kreuth – Germany
Ph: 01149–8029–8235
      (Clinic)
      01149–8029–8765
      (private)
Fax: 01149–8029–8378
      (Clinic)
      01149–8029–8888
      (personal)

Bede Griffiths International
  Trust Archives
Incarnation Monastery
Br Cassian Hardie O.S.B. Cam.
1369 La Loma
USA – Berkeley, CA 94708
Ph: 001–510–548–0965
Fax: 001–510–845–0601